WEIGHT WATCHERS

New Complete Cookbook

#2024

1600 Days Quick Easy ww Recipes Eat Well and Reset Your Body with Simple, Super-Tasty Freestyle Smart Points

Lisa W Gardner

Table of Contents

INTRODUCTION

Welcome to "Deliciously Light: A Weight Watchers Cookbook." If you've picked up this book, you're embarking on a culinary journey that marries the pleasures of eating with the wisdom of wellness. We are thrilled to have you join us on this voyage towards a healthier, happier you.

At Weight Watchers, we've always believed in the transformative power of food. Food is more than sustenance; it's a source of joy, nourishment, and connection. With "Deliciously Light," we aim to show you that eating well can be both a pleasure and a path to improved well-being.

Hippocrates, the father of modern medicine, famously recognized the healing potential of food. In these pages, you'll discover recipes that embrace this philosophy, offering dishes that not only taste sensational but also align with the Weight Watchers program. Our goal is simple: to help you relish the journey to wellness.

Within these chapters, you'll encounter a delectable array of recipes suitable for every palate and every occasion. From quick and satisfying weeknight dinners to indulgent desserts for special moments, "Deliciously Light" has you covered. Our recipes include breakfasts that energize your day, lunches that fuel your afternoons, and dinners that leave you satisfied without compromise.

We understand that achieving a healthy lifestyle involves more than just counting calories. It's about making mindful choices, savoring every bite, and finding balance in your journey. That's why we've meticulously curated recipes that emphasize whole, unprocessed ingredients, and provided the SmartPoints values for each dish, empowering you to take control of your wellness.

"Deliciously Light" is not just a cookbook; it's your companion on a voyage towards a better you. It's about reimagining your relationship with food, celebrating its role in your life, and making it work for you.

As you embark on this culinary adventure, remember that you're not alone. Weight Watchers is a community of like-minded individuals, all striving for the same goal: a healthier, happier life. Together, we'll explore new flavors, celebrate the goodness of whole foods, and savor the journey to wellness.

So, let's dive into these recipes and savor the joy of cooking and eating, one delicious bite at a time. Here's to your well-being, your culinary adventure, and your brighter, healthier future!

Weight Watchers, now known as WW (Wellness that Works), is a popular and widely recognized weight loss and wellness program. It was founded in the 1960s by Jean Nidetch, and over the years, it has evolved to focus not just on weight loss but on overall health and well-being.

Here are the key components of the Weight Watchers program:

SmartPoints System: Weight Watchers assigns a point value to every food and beverage based on its nutritional content. These points are called "SmartPoints." Members are given a daily SmartPoints target based on their age, weight, height, and activity level. The goal is to stay within this daily point limit while still enjoying a variety of foods.

Food Tracking: Members are encouraged to track their food intake using the SmartPoints system. This helps them become more aware of their eating habits and make healthier choices.

ZeroPoint Foods: In addition to daily SmartPoints, Weight Watchers provides a list of "ZeroPoint" foods. These are foods that members can eat without counting points. These foods are typically high in protein and low in saturated fat and sugar, encouraging the consumption of healthier options.

Support and Community: Weight Watchers emphasizes the importance of support and community. Members can attend in-person meetings, join virtual workshops, or use the online tools and app to track their progress and connect with others on the same journey.

Personalized Plans: The program offers different plans to cater to various dietary preferences and lifestyles. These plans may include variations like the Green Plan, Blue Plan, and Purple Plan, each with its own list of ZeroPoint foods and SmartPoints system.

Physical Activity: Weight Watchers also encourages physical activity as an essential component of a healthy lifestyle. Members can earn FitPoints for various activities and incorporate exercise into their wellness journey.

Wellness Focus: In recent years, Weight Watchers has shifted its focus from just weight loss to overall wellness. The program recognizes that health involves more than just the number on the scale and promotes a holistic approach to well-being.

Mindful Eating: Mindful eating practices are promoted to help members become more aware of their eating habits, make conscious choices, and enjoy their food without guilt.

Coaching and Resources: WW provides access to coaches and a wealth of resources, including recipes, meal planning tools, and educational content to support members in their wellness journey.

Weight Watchers has helped many people achieve their weight loss and wellness goals by offering a flexible and sustainable approach to healthier living. It has evolved over the years to adapt to changing dietary preferences and scientific insights into nutrition and wellness. Please note that program details may have changed since my last knowledge update in September 2021, so it's advisable to check the latest information on the official WW website or consult with a WW representative for the most up-to-date details.

Dairy Free Butternut Squash Soup

Prep Time 10 Minutes

Cook Time 5 Minutes

Total Time 15 Minutes

Serving Size: 3

Equipment
- Stock Pot
- Immersion Blender
- Vitamix Blender

Ingredients
- 1 butternut squash medium, diced – about 2 1/2 cups
- 1 yellow onion diced
- 1 tbsp butter Earth Balance Dairy Free butter
- 1 tsp paprika
- 30 oz. vegetable stock low sodium
- 2 tbsp coconut cream optional (can also use heavy cream, it's just not vegan or dairy free)
- salt and pepper to taste

Instructions
Butternut squash should be peeled and cut into 1-inch pieces.

Slice the onion whole.

Melt Earth Balance "butter" in a big pot.

Cook the onions for about 2 minutes or until they are translucent.

Cook the butternut squash for a further two minutes after adding it.

Salt, pepper, paprika, and vegetable stock should all be added.

Simmer the butternut squash for a while, covered. Add everything to a sizable mixing basin.

Blend the ingredients until they are smooth with a hand mixer. If serving immediately, add cream. If not, add the cream just before serving and after rewarming. Decorate as desired.

PowerPoints 4 | 3 Blue Plan Points | 3 Green Plan Points | 3 Purple Plan Points | 5 Smart Points

Instant Pot Coconut Rice

Prep Time 2 Minutes

Cook Time 24 Minutes

Serving Size: 12

Equipment
- Instant Pot 6 qt
- Coconut Milk
- Olive Oil Spray

Ingredients
- Brown rice, 2 cups I employ quick grain.
- To make 2 cups of liquid, blend 1 full-fat coconut milk with 1 can of water.

Instructions

Your first step should be to rinse your rice in cool water. Ensure the water runs clean and you give it a thorough rinsing.

After that, add the rinsed rice to your electric pressure cooker and coat the interior pot with cooking oil spray.

You must now add the same amount of liquid (2 cups = 2 cups) to your rice. Fill a measuring cup with water until it holds 2 cups, then add the full-fat coconut milk.

To your instant pot, add water and coconut milk.

Turn the pressure release valve to the Sealing position and close the pot's lid.

Set the cooking time to 24 minutes using the Manual or Pressure Cook buttons.

Let any leftover pressure freely release after the cooking period has ended. Turn off the "keep warm" setting if your pot has one, and give the natural release process at least 10 minutes to complete. Rice will only stick to the bottom of the pool if the Pressure is released naturally with heat.

PowerPoints 7

Crispy Air Fryer Tofu

Prep Time 20 Minutes

Cook Time 20 Minutes

Marinade Time 15 Minutes

Total Time 55 Minutes

Serving Size: 4

Equipment
- Ninja Foodi
- Tofu Press
- Cutting Board

Ingredients
- 1 14 oz Extra Firm Tofu
- ½ cup
- 2 tbsp Sesame Seeds Optional

Instructions

Use a tofu press or some heavy pots or pans to press the extra water out of the block. Depending on how aggressive you are with adding weight and tightening the press, this usually takes 20 to 30 minutes.

Slice into thin (1/4 inch strips is what we're going for) strips.

Sliced tofu and the desired amount of sauce should be placed in a large bowl.

As long as you have before you start cooking, let the tofu marinate for 10 to 20 minutes. You'll have more flavored tofu the longer you let it marinate.

Apply some cooking spray made with olive oil to the bottom of your air fryer basket. On the bottom of the fryer, arrange the tofu pieces in a single layer.

Set the air fryer to 375 degrees and cook the food for 10 to 20 minutes, checking on it every five minutes.

Your tofu should be turned over after 10 minutes of cooking. Flipping them helps ensure they are cooked evenly because the bottom always browns a little more quickly.

When the tofu pieces are golden brown, remove them and, if necessary, add more sauce. If you'd like, sprinkle sesame seeds on top.

Healthy Dill Pickle Chicken Salad

Prep Time 10 Minutes

Cook Time 12 Minutes

Total Time 22 Minutes

Serving 6

Equipment
- Instant Pot 6 qt
- Kitchen Knife
- Cutting Board

Ingredients
- 1 pound chicken breast, about 2 breasts
- 1/3 cup vinegar. I use white
- 1 cup dill pickles chopped; please see note in post about using 1/2 pickles and 1/2 cucumbers
- 3/4 cup plain Greek yogurt. I prefer 2%
- 3/4 cup cottage cheese
- 1 tbsp fresh parsley chopped (or 1 tsp dried)
- 1/2 tbsp fresh dill chopped (or 1/2 tsp dried)
- 1 tbsp fresh chives chopped (or 1 tsp dried)
- 1 tsp garlic
- 1 tsp black pepper

Instructions
Directions for the Instant Pot:

To the Instant Pot insert, add the chicken and vinegar.

Turn the pressure valve to Sealing before closing the lid. For 10–12 minutes, cook the chicken under high Pressure using the manual or pressure cook option. Before doing a fast release, allow the pressure to release naturally for at least 10 minutes.

Blend or process the Greek yogurt, cottage cheese, garlic, and pepper until completely smooth.

Add the chicken to the food processor after removing the lid from the blender. The chicken breasts might need to be cut in half to fit.

The chicken should be shredded with the sauce using a food processor or blender. The chicken may be sliced in 5 to 15 seconds.

Remove the lid, then take out the blade. Combine the dip with the chives, dill, parsley, and dill pickles. Serve with garnish and cut vegetables for dipping.

Using the Stove Top:

To a saucepan, add the chicken and vinegar.

Put a lid on the saucepan and simmer the chicken for 15-20 minutes at medium-high heat or until it is thoroughly cooked.

Greek yogurt, cottage cheese, garlic, and pepper should be blended or processed until smooth.

Add the chicken to the food processor after removing the lid from the blender. The chicken breasts might need to be split in half to fit.

The chicken should be shredded with the sauce using a food processor or blender. The chicken may be sliced in 5 to 15 seconds.

Remove the lid, then take out the blade. Combine the dip with the chives, dill, parsley, and dill pickles. Serve with garnish and cut vegetables for dipping.

Simmering Pot Directions:

Vinegar and chicken should be added to your slow cooker.

Cook the chicken in the slow cooker on high heat for two to three hours, then on low heat for four to five hours or until thoroughly cooked.

Blend or process the Greek yogurt, cottage cheese, garlic, and pepper until completely smooth.

Add the chicken to the food processor after removing the lid from the blender. The chicken breasts might need to be split in half to fit.

The chicken should be shredded with the sauce using a food processor or blender. The chicken may be sliced in 5 to 15 seconds.

Remove the lid, then take out the blade. Combine the dip with the chives, dill, parsley, and dill pickles. Serve garnished with sliced vegetables for dipping.

PowerPoints 1 Blue Plan Point, 2 Green Plan Points, and 1 Purple Plan Point

Healthy Crack Chicken Casserole with Rice

Prep Time 10 Minutes

Cook Time 25 Minutes

Total Time 35 Minutes

Serving Size: 4

Equipment
- Instant Pot 6 qt
- Sealing Rings
- Kitchen Knife

Ingredients
- 1.5 lbs frozen chicken breast (frozen for Instant Pot method because it takes extra time to cook the dry rice)
- 2 cloves garlic minced
- 1 tsp onion powder
- 1 tsp dill dried
- 1 tsp parsley dried
- 1/2 tsp pepper
- 1 cup brown rice dry
- 1 cup chicken broth low sodium, 2 cups if cooking on the stovetop
- 3/4 cup Greek yogurt plain, 2%
- 2/3 cup cheddar cheese shredded
- 8 slices turkey bacon cooked and chopped

Instructions
Instant Pot:

Set your pot insert to saute after lightly spraying it with cooking spray.

One layer of bacon should be used. 3–5 minutes on one side of the pan. Once cooked through and the sides have started curling, flip your bacon over and fry for 3–5 minutes. Move the bacon to a platter covered with paper towels to drain any extra grease. Chop your bacon into little pieces after it is cold enough to handle.

Place your frozen chicken in the bottom of your pot after cleaning it, if desired.

On top of your chicken, sprinkle the dried dill, parsley, garlic, onion powder, and black pepper from the ranch spice mix.

Place the brown rice on the opposite side of your saucepan from the frozen chicken breast.

Over the brown rice, pour the chicken broth (or 1 cup of water).

Turn the pressure valve handle to Sealing before closing the lid. Set your high-pressure cook time to 25 minutes.

If your "keep warm" button is on, turn it off when the cooking time is up.

Permit the pot's Pressure to release gradually.

Remove the Instant Pot cover when the pressure valve decreases or after 15 minutes.

Take the chicken out of the pot and shred it with two forks (or a stand mixer, if you prefer.

Stir the chicken and rice together before returning the shredded chicken to the pot.

Once the pot contents have cooled for a few minutes, stir in the Greek yogurt, cheese, and cooked turkey bacon.

To thoroughly incorporate all ingredients, stir well. As desired, garnish with more cheddar cheese and green onions. Serve hot.

For preparation on the hob, the chicken must first be defrosted.

Once the bacon has cooled, slice it into little pieces after cooking it as directed on the box.

On the stove, heat a sizable skillet over high heat. Add the chicken, dill, parsley, black pepper, onion powder, garlic, and onion powder.

Two cups of chicken broth should be added. Stir in the brown rice after bringing the liquid to a boil.

Turn down the heat and cover the skillet. Stir the rice and chicken occasionally to prevent scorching throughout the 40–50 minutes simmering period.

Use two forks or a stand mixer to shred the chicken once it is done cooking (internal temperature reaches 165°F).

Take the skillet from the stove. Add the cheese, bacon, and Greek yogurt while the chicken and rice are still heated. Before serving, let it sit for approximately 5 minutes.

Slow cooker:

To prepare this in a slow cooker, your chicken must first be thawed.

Once the bacon has cooled, slice it into little pieces after cooking it as directed on the box.

Add the chicken, garlic, onion powder, pepper, dill, and parsley to the slow cooker insert.

After placing the chicken on top of the To make brown rice, you will need to Please add one and a half cups of chicken broth.

Rice and chicken should be prepared after 2-3 hours of high-heat cooking in a covered slow cooker.

Take off the lid, and using two forks or a stand mixer, shred the chicken. Add the cheese, bacon, and Greek yogurt after that.

Before serving, give your casserole about 10 minutes to rest.

PowerPoints 8 Blue Plan Points 11 Green Plan Points | 3 Purple Plan Points

Healthy Crockpot Jambalaya with Quinoa

Prep Time 15 Minutes

Cook Time 7 hours

Total Time 7 hours HRS 15 Minutes

Serving Size: 6

Equipment

- Crockpot
- Kitchen Knife
- Strainer

Ingredients

- 1½ cups chopped onion
- 1½ cups chopped celery
- 4 cloves garlic minced
- 1 lb chicken breast
- 1 lb chicken sausage Low sodium
- 30 oz diced tomatoes
- 1 tsp thyme
- 1 tsp oregano
- 1 tsp red pepper crushed
- 1 tsp Tabasco sauce
- 1 lb cooked shrimp peeled, deveined, tails removed
- 1 tsp basil
- 3 cups quinoa
- Optional topping: diced green onions

Instructions

Chop the celery, onions, and garlic.

Sausage should be sliced into half-inch-thick slices, and chicken breasts should be cut into one-inch squares.

Stir well before adding the diced tomatoes, crushed red pepper, thyme, oregano, onions, celery, garlic, chicken, and sausage to the crockpot.

Cook the chicken for 6-7 hours on low Cook the food until its internal temperature reaches 165°F.

Cook your quinoa when your crockpot's cook cycle is almost through. Your quinoa should be rinsed before being added to a pot of water. Bring the water to a boil over high heat before covering the saucepan. Stirring occasionally, simmer for 15 to 20 minutes over low heat. 1 cup of quinoa to 2 cups of liquid is the standard ratio. For this quinoa jambalaya, 3 cups of cooked quinoa are required.

Add the cooked quinoa, basil, and prawns at this point. Cover the pan and continue cooking as soon as the shrimp and quinoa are heated.

Serve with freshly cut green onions after thoroughly stirring.

PowerPoints 5 | 6 Blue Plan Points | 8 Green Plan Points | 3 Purple Plan Points

Weight Watchers Beef Enchiladas

Prep Time 15 Minutes

Cook Time 20 Minutes

Total Time 35 Minutes

Serving 6

Equipment
- Baking Dish
- Vitamix Blender
- Kitchen Knife

Ingredients
- Ingredients in Enchiladas
- 12 corn tortillas
- 1 Pounds carne Asada or meat of your choice
- 2 cups shredded cheese reduced fat
- ½ cups enchilada sauce
- Ingredients in Carne Asada
- 1.5 Pounds of skirt steak diced into small pieces
- ¼ cup white vinegar
- 2 tbsp low sodium tamari or soy sauce
- 1 tsp garlic powder
- 2 tbsp lime juice from 1 lime
- 2 tsp olive oil
- juice from 1 orange fresh squeezed
- 1 tbsp chili powder
- 1 tsp oregano
- 1 tsp cumin
- 1 tsp onion powder
- Ingredients in Red Enchilada Sauce
- 20 Colorado (Red) Chile Pods dried, stemmed, and seeded
- 3 cups water
- ¼ cup white vinegar
- 1 tsp oregano
- ½ tsp allspice
- 1 tsp garlic powder
- 1 tsp onion powder

Instructions
Turn on the oven to 350 degrees.

Put a little oil on just the bottom of a casserole pan.

After greasing the skillet, use ¼ cup of enchilada sauce to cover the bottom.

Put some cheese and carne asada meat in the center of a corn tortilla before rolling the enchiladas. For my own, I use 1/3 cup cheese for four enchiladas and 3/4 cup meat for two tortillas.

You must lay each enchilada down individually and fold the side over to fill an entire pan. To have more of a "flap" to fold over the top, I think it helpful to lay the filling slightly off-center with the seam side down in the pan.

Sprinkle the remaining cheese on top after adding the final 3/4 cup of enchilada sauce.

For 20 to 25 minutes, these delectable Weight Watchers enchiladas should bake. You'll know they're ready to come out when the cheese looks melty and a little crunchy. Serve garnished with fresh cilantro!

Guidelines for cooking Carne Asada

Slice or dice the steak thinly first.

The next step is to combine all the marinade ingredients in a sizable lidded bag or container.

Then, add the diced steak to the container and stir to ensure that the marinade is evenly distributed throughout.

Place for at least an hour or overnight in the refrigerator.

Place a sizable skillet over medium-high heat and coat with avocado or olive oil. Scoop the meat into the skillet once heated, and discard the marinade.

Cook the meat for the necessary amount of time (at least 145°F for the internal temperature). (8 to 10 minutes)

When you're prepared to assemble your enchiladas, Take the carne asada off the heat and place it in a separate dish.

the recipe for the enchilada sauce

A sizable saucepan should be filled with the ingredients for the enchilada sauce.

Over high heat, bring the sauce to a boil. After that, lower the heat to medium and let the chili pods simmer for 15 to 20 minutes or until tender.

After allowing the chili pods to cool, pour the entire sauce pan's contents into a blender. Blend the sauce up to smoothness.

Use the sauce immediately, or keep it in the freezer or refrigerator until you're ready. The sauce can be frozen for up to a month and held in the fridge for 5-7 days.

PowerPoints 11 Blue Plan Points | 11 Green Plan Points | 11 Purple Plan Points

Instant Pot Honey Garlic Chicken

Prep Time 15 Minutes

Cook Time 14 Minutes

Total Time 29 Minutes

Serving 4

Equipment
- Instant Pot 6 qt
- Kitchen Knife
- Cutting Board

Ingredients
- 3/4 cup uncooked white quinoa rinsed
- 1 cup water
- 1 tbsp minced garlic
- 1/4 cup honey
- 2 tbsp Coconut aminos or reduced-sodium soy sauce
- 2 tsp chili garlic sauce or 1 tsp crushed red pepper flakes
- 1 1/2 pounds chicken thighs boneless, skinless
- 4 cups broccoli florets chopped

Instructions

Apply cooking spray containing olive oil to the inner pot. 1 cup of water and the rinsed quinoa should be added to the inner saucepan.

Lock the lid by closing it. Specify a 1-minute (high-pressure) cook time. Allow the Pressure to naturally release for 10 minutes after the cooking process is finished before quickly releasing any leftover pressure. Quinoa is removed and left aside.

Thoroughly mix the garlic, honey, coconut aminos, and chili garlic sauce in a small bowl.

Reapply the cooking spray with olive oil. Put the chicken in the pot and cover it with the sauce.

Set the cooking time to 12 Minutes (High Pressure) and shut the lid. Quickly release the Pressure and remove the top after the cooking period. Slice the cooked chicken into bite-sized pieces on a chopping board.

Add the broccoli to the pot, and then add the trivet. If any of the bits fall through and hit the bottom of the pool, that's okay.

Set the cooking time to 1 minute and securely fasten the cover. Use a rapid pressure release after the cooking time is finished, and then take off the lid.

With oven mitts, remove the trivet from the bottom of the instant pot, then add the broccoli and the diced chicken, stirring to distribute the leftover sauce evenly.

Top the cooked quinoa with the chicken and broccoli mixture on a platter or bowl to serve.

PowerPoints 11 Blue Plan Points | 11 Green Plan Points | 8 Purple Plan Points | 9 Points

Nutrition

Calories: 430kcal | Carbohydrates: 47g | Protein: 40g | Fat: 9g | Saturated Fat: 2g | Polyunsaturated Fat: 3g | Monounsaturated Fat: 3g | Trans Fat: 0.03g | Cholesterol: 162mg | Sodium: 472mg | Potassium: 903mg | Fiber: 5g | Sugar: 21g | Vitamin A: 612IU | Vitamin C: 82mg | Calcium: 80mg | Iron: 4mg

Instant Pot Ramen Stir Fry with Chicken

Prep Time 15 Minutes

Cook Time 13 Minutes

Total Time 28 Minutes

Serving Size: 4

Equipment
- Instant Pot 6 qt
- Cutting Board
- Kitchen Knife

Ingredients
- ½ cup or low sodium soy sauce
- 3 tbsp minced ginger root
- 1 tbsp sesame oil Roasted sesame oil has the best flavor
- 1 ½ tsp rice vinegar, no additional sweeteners
- 1 tsp minced garlic fresh is best
- 1 tsp black pepper
- 1 tsp crushed red pepper, optional
- 1 tsp molasses
- 3 tbsp honey
- 1 ½ pounds boneless, skinless chicken thighs
- ¾ cup water
- 6 cups chopped broccoli
- 2 cups white button mushrooms chopped
- 4 cakes of brown rice ramen or 20 oz wheat spaghetti noodles
- 2 tsp sesame seeds

Instructions
Apply cooking spray containing olive oil to the inner pot.

Coconut aminos, ginger root, sesame oil, rice vinegar, garlic, black pepper, optional crushed red pepper, molasses, and honey should all be combined in a blender. Mix until well combined.

Half of the sauce should be poured over the chicken thighs in the pot; save the other half for another use. Fill the pot with water.

After sealing the Instant Pot's lid, turn the steam release handle to the sealing position. Choose Pressure Using the high setting, cook for 12 minutes.

Broccoli and mushrooms should be combined in a big bowl, and the leftover sauce should be poured over the veggies. Cook the chicken as usual until the chicken is finished, and set aside.

Once the chicken has finished cooking, quickly reduce the Pressure and remove the lid.

Do not drain the cooking liquid from the pot before transferring the chicken thighs to a large bowl. The chicken should be shredded with two forks, then set aside.

Put the spaghetti noodles or ramen cakes in the bottom of the pot with the cooking liquid, followed by the vegetables and sauce.

Lock the lid, then turn the steam release handle to the sealing position. Choose Pressure. Set the cooking time to one minute and select Cook (High). Quickly release the pressure and remove the lid after the cooking period.

Use tongs to combine the noodles, chicken, and vegetables in the saucepan before adding the sesame seeds.

PowerPoints 11 | 14 Blue Plan Points | 17 Green Plan Points | 7 Purple Points

Healthy Pork and Beans

Prep Time 5 Minutes

Cook Time 45 Minutes

Total Time 50 Minutes

Serving Size 4

Equipment
- Stock Pot
- Instant Pot 6 qt
- Enameled Cast Iron Pan

Ingredients
- 1 can white beans 14 oz can, undrained. I used great northern beans
- 8 slices bacon turkey or nitrate-free | cooked, but not crispy. Cut into small pieces.
- 1 tsp onion powder
- ¼ tsp smoked paprika
- 1 tsp molasses
- 1 tsp garlic powder
- ¼ cup honey

Instructions
Stove Top

First, cook the bacon. You want to be cooked, not crispy, bacon for this recipe.

Next, add all ingredients into a medium saucepan or large skillet over medium-high heat. I always spray my pans with olive oil before cooking; if you're nervous about sticking, you can also use olive oil.

Then lower the temperature, cover the pan, and allow the pork and beans to simmer for 45 Minutes, stirring a few times so the beans don't stick. If you like a thick sauce, I will remove the top so some moisture can escape. If you're not worried about stale beans, I'd leave the lid on.

After the beans are cooked, and the sauce has thickened, you can remove the pan from the heat and serve immediately.

Instant Pot

Add all ingredients (cooked bacon included) to the Instant Pot or pressure cooker.

Close the lid and turn the pressure valve to Sealing.

Then set the Instant Pot on high Pressure (or manual setting) for 3 Minutes.

When cooking is done, quickly release the Pressure and stir the beans.

Serve immediately or store in an airtight container.

PowerPoints 7 | 6 Blue Points | 9 Green Points | 6 Purple Points

Weight Watchers Buffalo Chicken Dip

Prep Time 5 Minutes

Cook Time 15 Minutes

Total Time 20 Minutes

Serving 8

Equipment
- Instant Pot 6 qt
- Sealing Rings
- Food processor

Ingredients
- 2 lbs chicken breasts frozen
- ¾ cup cottage cheese 1%
- ¾ cup Greek yogurt plain fat-free
- ½ tsp garlic powder
- ½ tsp onion powder
- ½ tsp dried dill
- ½ tsp dried parsley
- ¼ tsp black pepper
- ¾ cup hot sauce Frank's Hot Sauce, not buffalo sauce
- Optional toppings: Shredded cheddar cheese, goat cheese, green onions

Instructions
Instant Pot:

Add your frozen chicken breasts to the Instant Pot and cover with 1 cup of water. Close and lock the lid and turn the pressure valve to Sealing. Select Pressure Cook (high) and set the cooking time for 12 Minutes.

Add cottage cheese, greek yogurt, garlic powder, onion powder, dill, parsley, black pepper, and Frank's Hot Sauce to your blender or food processor. Blend on high until well combined and smooth. This will take about a minute. You may have to stop and scrape the sides to mix evenly.

Once the cooking time is complete, allow the pressure to release naturally. When the pressure valve drops, remove the lid. Drain and shred your chicken. I love using a stand mixer to slice it, but two forks also work.

Turn your Instant Pot to Sauté and add the contents of your blender. Once the sauce bubbles, turn off the heat and add your shredded chicken.

Top as desired with shredded cheese, goat cheese, or green onions. Serve immediately or refrigerate and serve cold. This is a great recipe for meal prep. Place individual servings in separate containers and refrigerate or freeze until ready to eat.

Crockpot:

Place chicken in the crockpot and cook on high for 4 hours.

While your chicken cooks, prepare your buffalo ranch sauce by adding cottage cheese, greek yogurt, garlic powder, onion powder, dill, parsley, black pepper, and Frank's Hot Sauce to your blender or food processor. Blend on high until well combined and smooth. This will take about a minute. You may have to stop and scrape the sides to ensure all ingredients mix.

Shred your cooked chicken and stir in the sauce from your blender.

Top as desired with shredded cheese, goat cheese, or green onions and serve immediately or allow to chill in the refrigerator and serve cold.

Stovetop:

Place your chicken in a large pot and cover with water. Boil over high heat for about 20 Minutes or until chicken is cooked and reaches 165°F.

While your chicken cooks, prepare your buffalo ranch sauce by adding cottage cheese, greek yogurt, garlic powder, onion powder, dill, parsley, black pepper, and Frank's Hot Sauce to your blender or food processor. Blend on high until well combined and smooth. This will take about a minute. You may have to stop and scrape the sides to mix evenly.

Drain and shred your chicken and stir in the sauce from your blender.

Top as desired with shredded cheese, goat cheese, or green onions and serve immediately or allow to chill in the refrigerator and serve cold.

PowerPoints 0 | 0 Blue Plan Points | 3 Green Plan Points | 0 Purple Plan Points

Buffalo Cauliflower Dip with Chicken

Prep Time 5 Minutes

Cook Time 20 Minutes

Total Time 25 Minutes

Serving 8

Equipment
- Instant Pot 6 qt
- Vitamix Blender
- Kitchen Knife

Ingredients
- 1 tsp olive oil
- 1 Pounds chicken breast cut into bite-sized pieces
- 1/2 tsp garlic powder
- ½ tsp onion powder
- ¼ tsp black pepper
- ½ tsp dill dried
- ½ tsp parsley dried
- 1 head cauliflower cut into small bite-sized pieces
- ¾ cup Frank's Original Hot Sauce *not buffalo sauce
- 3/4 cup cottage cheese
- 3/4 cup plain Greek yogurt 2%
- 1 cup cheddar cheese shredded
- 2 tbsp brown rice flour

Instructions
Instant Pot Directions

Turn the Instant Pot to Sauté. Add the oil and allow it to heat up. When the oil is hot, add the chicken and sauté until the chicken is browned.

Add garlic powder, onion powder, black pepper, dill, and parsley to the pot. Mix up the chicken so that the seasoning is evenly distributed.

Add the cauliflower to the Instant Pot and cover with the hot sauce. The hot sauce acts as your liquid for this recipe. Close the lid and turn the pressure valve to Sealing.

Cook the chicken and cauliflower on high Pressure using the manual setting for 2 Minutes. Let the pressure release naturally for 6-10 Minutes before manually releasing it. This means that after the pot is done cooking, allow it to sit without touching it for 6-10 Minutes. The contents will still be cooking. After that time, move the Sealing valve to the Vent position and allow the steam to come out.

Mix together the contents of your pot, cottage cheese, and Greek yogurt in a high-speed blender to create a creamy sauce.

Blend the sauce until smooth, then add the cheese and brown rice flour. Blend until all is mixed and the cheese has melted. Serve with raw veggies or pita chips.

Stovetop Directions

Heat a large skillet on the stove and add the olive oil. When the oil is hot, sauté the chicken until it is browned.

Add the seasonings, hot sauce, and cauliflower to the skillet. Mix it up so the cauliflower is covered in hot sauce. Cover the skillet and reduce heat to medium-low heat.

Allow the cauliflower and chicken to cook for 10-15 Minutes, stirring occasionally until the cauliflower is very tender.

Blend the contents of the pan, cottage cheese, and Greek yogurt to make the sauce.

Add the cheddar cheese and brown rice flour into the blender until it melts together. Serve with raw veggies or pita chips.

Slow Cooker Directions

Add the chicken breast, cauliflower, seasoning, and hot sauce to the slower cooker.

Cover and let cook for 2 ½ to 4 hours on low heat or until the chicken is done and the cauliflower is soft.

Blend the contents of the slow cooker, cottage cheese, and Greek yogurt until smooth. Add the cheddar cheese and brown rice flour and blend until the cheese is melted. Serve with raw veggies or pita chips.

PowerPoints 1|3 Blue Plan Points | 4 Green Plan Points | 3 Purple Plan Points

Healthy Donuts in a Blender

Prep Time 10 Minutes

Cook Time 20 Minutes

Total Time 30 Minutes

Serving 2

Equipment
- Vitamix Blender
- donut pan
- Mixing Bowls

Ingredients
- 5 eggs
- ½ cup coconut milk
- ½ cup maple syrup
- ½ cup pumpkin puree
- ¼ cup coconut oil
- ¾ cup almond flour
- ½ cup coconut flour

Spices
- 1 tsp vanilla
- 1 tsp baking soda
- 1 tsp cinnamon
- ½ tsp nutmeg or ginger
- ¼ tsp cloves
- ¼ tsp salt

Instructions
Preheat the oven to 350 degrees.

Next, use nonstick spray to grease your doughnut pan's interior fully. I prepare this dish with coconut or avocado oil spray.

Combine the egg, coconut milk, pumpkin, and maple; Blend or process coconut oil and vanilla in a blender or food processor. Blend or process coconut oil and vanilla in a blender or food processor. Blend for about 15 seconds or until foamy.

Incorporate the dry ingredients at this point and combine on low for 10 to 20 seconds.

Pour the batter into the pan, filling each cavity 2/3 full. For 20 minutes, bake.

Allow the donuts to cool for 10 minutes after frying before removing them from the pan.

Run a knife over the edges of each donut to free it from the donut molds before removing it. To prevent the donut from breaking apart, lift it gently.

Apply tiny cooking oil spray to the donuts, then top with cinnamon and coconut crystals.

Let cool until room temperature, or merely reheat on a baking rack.

PowerPoints 7 | 8 Blue Plan Points | 9 Green Plan Points | 8 Purple Plan Points

Peanut Butter Lava Cake

Prep Time 10 Minutes

Cook Time 5 Minutes

Total Time 15 Minutes

Serving 7

Equipment
- Instant Pot 6 qt
- Egg Bite Molds
- Sealing Rings

Ingredients
- 4 tbsp butter or ghee
- 1/4 cup dark chocolate pieces
- 2 eggs
- 4 tbsp coconut milk or almond milk
- 1/3 cup brown rice flour or whole wheat flour
- 1/4 tsp salt
- 1 tbsp honey
- 1/2 tsp baking powder
- 1 tbsp cocoa powder
- 7 tsp peanut butter 1 tsp per lava cake

Optional toppings:
- coconut whip cream
- Stevia powdered
- raspberries
- Ingredients for coconut whipped cream:
- 1 can of coconut milk canned, refrigerated so that it is cold
- 1 tsp Stevia optional

Instructions
Combine butter and dark chocolate in a medium microwave-safe bowl (you may use semi-sweet if you don't mind the extra sugar). Stir to check if they are melting before adding another 30 seconds to the microwave to melt the butter and chocolate. It should take a minute.

Butter and chocolate should be combined with an electric mixer in a bowl.

Add the remaining ingredients (except the peanut butter): eggs, coconut milk, brown rice flour (You can also opt to use whole wheat flour instead. The other ingredients needed include salt, honey, baking powder, and cocoa powder. Blend the batter thoroughly.

Apply a thin layer of nonstick spray to Add an egg to each cup of your silicone egg bite mold. After greasing the cups, pour half the batter into each one.

The remaining cake mix should be poured into each cup after a spoonful of peanut butter is in the middle. Every cup needs to be filled up to the 3/4 mark.

Place the silicone mold on a trivet and cover it with foil.

Fill the Instant Pot inserts bottom with 1 cup of water. Using the handles, carefully lower the lava cakes into the Instant Pot with a trivet at the bottom.

Turn the pressure valve to Sealing as you close the lid. Use the Manual or Pressure Cook button to cook the lava cakes under high Pressure for 5 minutes. Take notes on how they turn out so you may alter the cooking time the next time you prepare these.

Quickly release the Pressure and remove the lava cakes from the Instant Pot when it beeps to indicate that the timer has expired. The pressure valve must be switched from Sealing to Venting manually using your finger or the end of a wooden spoon. Steam will emerge from the valve right away.

Remove the foil from the cakes while they are still hot, then carefully run a spoon down the rim of each cup to release them.

The lava cakes can be removed by placing a plate on them and turning them upside down.

Serve immediately with coconut whipped cream and strawberries, and top with powdered Stevia (optional).

Directions for Coconut Whipped Cream

After opening it, separate the milk from the cream in the coconut cream can. The milk should be liquid, and the cream should be firm.

Put the cream in a dish of ice. Substitute Stevia.

Use a hand mixer to beat the coconut cream for one to two minutes or until it is soft and resembles whipped cream.

Use it the same day, but keep it in the refrigerator until ready. The coconut whipped cream will last up to a day in the fridge.

PowerPoints 7 | 8 Blue Plan Points | 8 Green Plan Points | 8 Purple Plan Points

Hard Boiled Eggs

Prep Time 2 Minutes

Cook Time 5 Minutes

Total Time 7 Minutes

Serving 3

Equipment
- Instant Pot 6 qt
- Instant Pot Trivet
- Sealing Rings

Ingredients
- 6 Eggs
- 1 Cup Water (for 6 qt Instant Pot)

Instructions
Put a trivet or metal rack inside the pressure cooker.

Eggs are placed on the metal rack.

Fill the Instant Pot's bottom with 1 cup of water.

For five minutes, use the manual setting.

After releasing the Pressure and steam naturally for five minutes, physically remove the moisture.

Add hard-cooked eggs to a bowl of cold water.

Peel and enjoy.

PowerPoints 0 | 0 Blue Plan Points | 2 Green Plan Points | 0 Purple Plan Points

Healthy Air Fryer Eggplant

Prep Time 5 Minutes

Cook Time 25 Minutes

Total Time 30 Minutes

Serving 2

Equipment
- Ninja Foodi
- Kitchen Knife
- Cutting Board

Ingredients
- 1 eggplant medium
- 1 tbsp avocado oil
- ½ tsp black pepper ground
- ¼ tsp salt
- ½ tsp garlic powder

Instructions
Set your air fryer to 350°F.

Your eggplant should be cut into 1-inch cubes.

Toss your eggplant with avocado oil, pepper, salt, and garlic powder.

Set your air fryer for 25 minutes after adding the eggplant.

Every five minutes, shake your eggplant.

When the eggplant is soft and golden, it is finished.

PowerPoints 2 | Blue Plan Points: 2 | Green Plan Points: 2 | 2 Purple Plan Points

Healthy Egg Salad

Prep Time 4 Minutes

Cook Time 6 Minutes

Total Time 10 Minutes

Serving 4

Equipment
- Instant Pot 6 qt
- Kitchen Knife
- Cutting Board

Ingredients
- 8 eggs hard-boiled chopped
- ¾ cup plain yogurt
- 2 tsp mustard spicy brown
- ½ tsp paprika
- 1 tsp parsley
- ½ cup chopped celery
- optional: Salt and pepper to taste

Instructions
Instant Pot:

Crack the eggs into an oven-safe bowl that fits in the Instant Pot insert. Add 1 cup of water to the Instant Pot insert, then carefully lower the bowl of eggs to rest on the trivet. You can also hard-boil the eggs first, but this way is faster.

Close the lid and turn the pressure valve to Sealing. Cook on high Pressure for 6 minutes, then let the pressure release naturally.

Remove the lid and carefully lift the bowl from the Instant Pot. The bowl will be hot. Let the eggs cool to room temperature, then slice the eggs into cubes.

Mix in the yogurt, brown mustard, celery, paprika, parsley, and salt. Chill in their refrigerator until ready to serve.

Serve over a few leaves of lettuce and tomatoes to make a wrap.

Oven:

Preheat oven to 350 degrees F. Crack the eggs into an oven-safe bowl or pan. Bake the eggs for 20-25 Minutes until the yolks are cooked.

Remove the pan from the oven and let it cool.

Slice the eggs into cubes. Mix in the remaining ingredients. Chill the egg salad. Serve over leaves of lettuce and sliced tomatoes when ready.

Slow cooker:

Crack the eggs into an oven-safe bowl that fits inside your slow cooker. Add 2 cups water to the slow cooker and place the bowl of eggs into the slow cooker.

Cover the slow cooker with the lid. Cook the eggs on high heat for 1 1/2 – 2 hours. When the yolks are set, remove the bowl and let the eggs cool.

Slice the eggs into cubes. Mix in the remaining ingredients. Chill the egg salad until ready to serve. Serve over the leaves of lettuce and slices of tomatoes.

PowerPoints 0 | 0 Blue Plan Points | 5 Green Plan Points | 0 Purple Plan Points

Weight Watchers Turkey Sausage

Prep Time 10 Minutes

Cook Time 25 Minutes

Total Time 35 Minutes

Serving 4

Equipment
- Baking Sheet
- Slip Mat
- Mixing Bowls

Ingredients
- Sweet Breakfast Sausage
- 1 lb ground turkey or chicken
- 1 tsp cinnamon
- 1 tsp nutmeg
- ½ apple green, diced
- ¼ cup chicken bone broth low sodium
- Optional: salt to taste
- Savory Breakfast Sausage
- 1 lb ground turkey or chicken
- 3 tsp garlic
- ⅓ cup red onion
- 1 tsp cumin
- ½ tsp pepper
- ¼ cup bone broth low sodium
- Optional: salt to taste

Instructions
Combine the meat, stock, and seasonings in a big bowl. If you're preparing apple or onion sausage, dice them very finely because if they're too big, the sausage patties won't stick together well.

Then use your hands to combine the ingredients. Although you might be tempted to omit the bone broth, it provides additional nourishment and keeps these patties from drying up.

Form the sausage mixture into 12 tiny patties with your hands, then arrange them. To prepare a baking dish, you can line it with either parchment paper or a slipmat.

Sausage patties should be baked for around 25 minutes at 375 degrees. On average, I like to cook them for 10 minutes on each side.

PowerPoints 0 | 0 Blue Plan Points | 1 Green Plan Points | 0 Purple Plan Points

Weight Watchers Crack Chicken

Prep Time 5 Minutes

Cook Time 12 Minutes

Natural Release 10 Minutes

Total Time 27 Minutes

Serving 4

Equipment
- Instant Pot 6 qt
- Sealing Rings
- Olive Oil Spray

Ingredients
- 1 lb frozen chicken breast or thighs
- 4 slices of turkey bacon
- ¼ cup cheddar cheese fat-free
- ¾ cup cottage cheese fat-free
- ¼ cup Greek yogurt fat-free
- 1 tsp garlic salt
- 1 tsp onion powder
- ½ tsp pepper
- ½ tsp parsley
- 1 tsp fresh dill 1/2 tsp dried

Instructions
Instant Pot Directions:

Put the chicken (frozen or thawed) in the bottom of the Instant Pot. Lock the lid in place and switch the pressure valve to Seal after adding 1 cup of water.

Cook for 12 minutes at high pressure using the manual setting. When finished, allow the Pressure to dissipate naturally. By doing this, the chicken won't dry out.

Cook the turkey bacon in the oven as directed on the package while the chicken is cooking. Cut into cubes and hold back until required.

Combine the cottage cheese, yogurt, garlic salt, onion powder, pepper, parsley, and dill in a blender. Mix thoroughly until the dressing resembles ranch. Save for later use by setting aside.

The chicken is drained and shredded. Over the chicken, sprinkle cheddar cheese, turkey bacon, and the dressing from the blender. Mix thoroughly. If your chicken has cooled, you can switch the Instant Pot to sauté to aid in melting the cheese.

How to use a slow cooker

To the crockpot, add 1 cup of water or low-sodium chicken broth. Cook the chicken for four hours on high heat.

Cook the bacon in the oven while the chicken cooks. Once it has finished cooking, cube it.

Combine the cottage cheese, Greek yogurt, garlic salt, onion powder, pepper, parsley, and dill in a food processor or blender.

Your shredded chicken will receive the sauce. Add cheddar cheese and turkey bacon. Optional: If you want to keep it warm for later, add it back to the slow cooker.

Stovetop Directions:

To cook the chicken, bake or broil it. I favor putting it on the stove to boil.

The bacon should be cooked for around 15 minutes at 400 degrees. Cube it once it's finished.

Using two forks or a mixer, shred the chicken after cooking.

Combine the cottage cheese, Greek yogurt, garlic salt, onion powder, pepper, parsley, and dill in a food processor or blender.

Over the shredded chicken, pour the sauce. Cheddar cheese and fried bacon are added.

PowerPoints 0 | 1 Green Plan Point | 1 Blue Plan Point | 1 Purple Plan Point

Chicken Salad with Grapes

Prep Time 5 Minutes

Cook Time 5 Minutes

Total Time 10 Minutes

Serving 2

Equipment
- Crockpot
- Cutting Board
- Kitchen Knife

Ingredients
- 1 ½ cups cooked boneless skinless chicken breast chopped or shredded
- ½ cup seedless red grapes halved and chilled
- ½ cup seedless green grapes halved and chilled
- 1 small apple cored and diced
- ½ cup fat-free plain yogurt
- ⅛ tsp vanilla extract
- 1 tbsp olive oil mayo
- ¼ tsp black pepper
- 6 romaine or green tip lettuce leaves
- 10 pecans chopped

Instructions
Combine yogurt, mayo, vanilla essence, and pepper in a big bowl.

Add the sliced apple, half grapes, cooked and cut chicken, and chopped nuts.

Use right away, or chill first. Keep in the refrigerator for up to five days in an airtight container.

PowerPoints 3 | 5 Blue Plan Points | 8 Green Plan Points | 5 Purple Plan Points

Healthy Baked Beans Recipe with Ground Turkey

Prep Time 15 Minutes

Cook Time 1 hour

Total Time 1 hour HR 15 Minutes

Serving 12

Equipment
- Enameled Cast Iron Pan
- Kitchen Knife
- Cutting Board

Ingredients
- ¾ cup onions
- 1 can baked beans or homemade, 14 ounces
- 1 can dark red kidney beans 14 Ounces can
- 1 can black beans 14 Ounces can
- 1 Pound ground turkey or hamburger
- ½ cup brown sugar or honey
- 1 tablespoon dry mustard
- 2 teaspoons vinegar, apple cider, or white
- ⅓ cup ketchup low sugar

Instructions
Stove and Oven Directions

Dice and cook the onions in a large pan.

Add ground turkey to the onions in the pan.

While the turkey and onions are cooking, add the other ingredients to a large baking dish.

I drain the liquid from the beans, then set the juice aside if the beans look dry after cooking.

When meat and onions are cooked, drain if necessary, add the mixture to your baking dish, and mix well.

Cook at 350 degrees for an hour. If using a smoker, you can cook them in there for an hour–the flavor is delicious!

Instant Pot Instructions

Saute the meat and onions using the sauté function. Add 1/2 cup water.

Add all of the other ingredients to the Instant Pot.

Set on high Pressure (or manual) for 8 Minutes. Quick release and enjoy!

Frittata Recipe in Ramekins

Prep Time 2 Minutes

Cook Time 10 Minutes

Total Time 12 Minutes

Serving 3

Equipment
- Instant Pot 6 qt
- Ramekins
- Mixing Bowls

Ingredients
- 4 slices turkey bacon cooked and chopped
- 1 small red potato
- 1/2 bell pepper
- 1/2 small onion
- 6 eggs
- 1/4 cup milk
- 1/4 cup cheddar cheese
- salt & pepper to taste

Instructions
Cover the bottom of the ramekins with cooked and diced turkey bacon.

Then divide the vegetable mixture and arrange it in the ramekins on the bacon. Bacon, bell peppers, and onions are typically added first, followed by potatoes.

Then combine eggs, milk, salt, and pepper in a big bowl. After that, add the egg mixture to the vegetables. Shredded cheese should then be added.

Aluminum foil should be placed over each ramekin baking dish before setting it on the trivet with a cup of water in the bottom of the pot.

Your Instant Pot's lid should be locked, and the pressure release arm should be set to Sealing. Choose Pressure Cook (High Pressure) and enter 10 minutes for the cooking time.

Use the quick-release pressure technique to relieve the Pressure for the best outcomes. Observe as it cools.

PowerPoints 3

Healthy Cheesecake Recipe with Cottage Cheese

Prep Time 15 Minutes

Cook Time 35 Minutes

Total Time 50 Minutes

Serving 6

Equipment
- Instant Pot 6 qt
- Spring form Pan
- Instant Pot Trivet

Ingredients
Crust:

- 1/2 cup dry oatmeal
- 1 tbsp honey
- 1 tbsp unsalted butter melted
- Filling:
- 2 cups cottage cheese
- 1/2 cup Greek yogurt plain or vanilla
- 2 eggs
- 3 tbsp honey
- 1 tbsp rice flour
- 1 tsp vanilla extract
- 1/2 cup strawberries sliced

Instructions

Add 2 cups of water to the pot before adding the trivet. Set aside a round oven-safe dish or spring form pan coated with nonstick cooking spray.

Add muesli, 1 tablespoon of honey, and melted butter to your food processor. Blend until a dough starts to form and the grains are finely chopped. The crust mixture should be poured into an oiled pan and pressed firmly into the pan's bottom. The crust can be compacted using the glass's base.

After cleaning and drying it, put rice flour, vanilla essence, eggs, cottage cheese, Greek yogurt, and 3 tablespoons of honey into the food processor. The filling should be smooth after 5 minutes of blending. It will be wet.

W carefully wrap the pan in foil after spreading the filling over the crust. Lower into your pot slowly. Turn the pressure release arm to sealing as you close and lock the lid. Thirty-five minutes is the cooking time setting for the pressure cook on high.

Allow your Pressure to naturally release after the cooking period is finished. Remove the cover and place your cheesecake in the refrigerator when the pressure valve opens. Overnight rest is advised.

Strawberries should be cut into six equal slices and garnished when the dish is ready to be served.

Chicken Gyro Bowl with Homemade Tzatziki

Prep Time 10 Minutes

Cook Time 15 Minutes

Total Time 25 Minutes

Serving 6

Equipment
- Instant Pot 6 qt
- Enameled Cast Iron Pan
- Crockpot

Ingredients
- Chicken Gyro Bowls
- 1 spaghetti squash, about 3 lbs.
- 1 – 1.5 lbs chicken thighs, about 6 thighs, defrosted
- 2 tsp olive oil
- 1/2 tbsp garlic powder
- 1 tsp oregano dried
- 1 tsp rosemary dried
- 1/2 tsp pepper
- 1/2 cup basil fresh, chopped
- 1 red onion, chopped
- 1 cucumber sliced
- 1 cup cherry tomatoes cut in half
- Homemade Tzatziki Sauce
- 3/4 cup Greek yogurt plain, 2%
- 1 cup cucumber peeled, seeded, and chopped
- 1 clove garlic minced
- 1 tsp pepper
- 2 tbsp fresh dill

Instructions
Instant Pot:

Scoop out the seeds from the center of the spaghetti squash after cutting it in half.

Combine all the chicken ingredients in a sizable bowl. Olive oil and seasoning should completely cover the chicken.

Sauté is selected on the Instant Pot. Sauté the chicken for 2-3 minutes on each side after the Instant Pot is hot. Remove and reserve the chicken.

Place the trivet on the bottom of the Instant Pot insert and add 1 cup of water. Set the chicken all over the spaghetti squash and set it on top of the trivet.

Cook for 10 minutes under high Pressure using the manual setting after closing the lid and allowing the pressure to release naturally.

Chicken and spaghetti squash should be taken out. While the spaghetti squash cools, chop the chicken. Once the spaghetti squash is cold, To easily extract the "noodles," one can use a fork to handle and scrape them out." They ought to open up straight now.

Put the spaghetti squash on the bottom of your bowls, then add the diced chicken, cucumbers, tomatoes, red onions, basil, and Tzatziki sauce on top.

Stovetop and Oven:

Set the oven's temperature to 400. Scoop out the seed after cutting the spaghetti squash in half. Squash should be placed cut side down on a baking sheet. 30 to 45 minutes of baking.

Combine all the chicken ingredients in a sizable bowl. Olive oil and seasoning should completely cover the chicken.

On the stove, preheat a skillet over medium-high heat. After browning the chicken for 2-3 minutes on each side, turn the heat to medium and continue cooking it for an additional 10–12 minutes or until it is fully cooked. Chicken is taken off the fire and is diced.

After cooking the spaghetti squash, let it cool before removing the "noodles."

Put the spaghetti squash on the bottom of your bowls, then add the diced chicken, cucumbers, tomatoes, red onions, basil, and Tzatziki sauce on top.

Slice the spaghetti squash in half, then remove the seeds in the slow cooker. Put the squash in the slow cooker and cut side down.

Combine all the chicken ingredients in a sizable bowl. Olive oil and seasoning should completely cover the chicken.

On the stove, preheat a skillet over medium-high heat. The chicken should be browned for a few minutes on each side before being placed in the slow cooker. Around the spaghetti squash, arrange the chicken.

Place ½ cup of water in the slow cooker and then secure the top. Cook for 4-6 hours on low heat or 2-3 hours on high heat.

Before removing the spaghetti squash noodles, remove it and let it cool. Prepare the chicken for dicing and put the spaghetti squash in each bowl before adding the chicken, basil, cucumbers, tomatoes, red onions, and Tzatziki sauce.

PowerPoints 0 | 0 Blue Plan Points | 2 Green Plan Points | 0 Purple Plan Points.

Bacon Wrapped BBQ Meatloaf Bombs

Prep Time 15 Minutes

Cook Time 15 Minutes

Pressure Release 8 Minutes

Total Time 38 Minutes

Serving 8

Equipment
- Instant Pot 6 qt
- Baking Sheet
- Crockpot

Ingredients
BBQ Sauce

- 1 cup tomato paste
- 1/2 cup water
- 1/4 cup honey
- 1/4 cup apple cider vinegar
- 1 tsp hot sauce
- 1 tsp smoked paprika
- 2 tbsp
- 1 tsp minced garlic
- 1/8 tsp cumin
- 1 tbsp mustard

Meatballs:

- 2 lbs ground turkey or ground beef
- 1 tbsp oregano
- 1 tsp pepper
- 1 tbsp Coconut Aminos low sodium
- 1 egg
- 2 onions end cut off and separated, medium-large yellow. You may need more depending on how many you're making
- 16 slices of turkey bacon

Instructions
Instant Pot:

Mix all the ingredients for the BBQ sauce in a medium bowl.

Next, trim the ends from your onions. After that, cut a slit halfway across the onion's center to remove the soft outer layers. Peel the onion and separate the layers. 8 more giant onion rings are required.

Combine all of the meatball ingredients in a big bowl. Meatballs should be measured and formed using a red container (or a 3/4 cup measuring cup). After placing the meatballs into the onion shells, take two pieces of bacon and wrap the onion bombs with bacon.

Place four meatballs on each layer of the bacon-wrapped BBQ meatloaf bombs in a stackable steamer. After covering each meatball with sauce, cover the heating container.

The trivet and the Instant Pot insert should have 2 cups of water in the bottom. Close the Instant Pot cover while turning the pressure valve to Sealing, then place the steaming rack on the trivet.

Cook the meatballs under high Pressure for 15–18 minutes (I cooked mine for 15) using the manual setting. Let the Pressure generally relax for around 8 minutes after the cooking time. Serve the meatballs topped with any additional sauce you have on hand, and remove the heating rack from the Instant Pot.

The slow cooker

Combine all the ingredients for the BBQ sauce in a medium bowl.

Next, trim the ends from your onions. After that, cut a slit halfway across the onion's center to remove the soft outer layers. Peel the onion and separate the layers. 8 more giant onion rings are required.

In a sizable mixing bowl, mix all the meatball ingredients. Meatballs should be measured and formed using a red container (or a ¾ cup measuring cup). Each meatball is encased in an onion layer.

In the slow cooker, add onion bombs, cover, and then top each meatball with sauce. Cook for 3-5 hours on high or 6-8 hours on low.

Please take out the bacon bombs and serve them with any additional sauce.

Oven

Mix all the ingredients for the BBQ sauce in a medium bowl.

Next, trim the ends from your onions. After that, cut a slit halfway across the onion's center to remove the soft outer layers. Peel the onion and separate the layers. 8 more giant onion rings are required.

Combine all of the meatball ingredients in a big bowl. Meatballs should be measured and formed using a red container (or a ¾ cup measuring cup). After placing the meatballs into the onion shells, wrap the onion bombs in two slices of bacon.

Place the meatballs on a baking sheet or dish prepared with parchment paper, cover with foil, and then top each meatball with sauce. Cook at 425 degrees Fahrenheit for 40 minutes.

Remove the bacon bombs and serve with any remaining sauce after the cooking time is over.

PowerPoints 5

Buffalo Chicken Roll-Ups with Cottage Cheese

Prep Time 20 Minutes

Cook Time 20 Minutes

Total Time 40 Minutes

Serving 4

Equipment
- Ninja Foodi
- Kitchen Knife
- Food processor

Ingredients
- 1 ¼ Pounds chicken breast cutlets (I used four cutlets)
- 1 cup cottage cheese rinsed
- 3/4 tsp dill
- 3/4 tsp onion powder
- 3/4 tsp parsley
- 3/4 tsp garlic powder
- ½ cup hot sauce. I used Frank's
- 1/3 cup cheddar jack cheese shredded
- 1/4 tsp black pepper or chili pepper optional
- 12 Pieces spinach (2-3 for each piece of chicken)
- 1 egg optional for helping breadcrumbs stick
- 1.5 cups breadcrumbs whole wheat

Instructions
Make cutlets from your chicken by filleting it; I cut mine in half. As much as you can, flatten the chicken with a meat tenderizer. Rolling is made simpler by this. I use the flat side of the tenderizer and place parchment paper on top of the chicken.

Combine the spices and cottage cheese in a food processor. The cottage cheese becomes smooth after being blended in this way. To combine everything, add the hot sauce and pulse once more.

If you're using one for this stage, I recommend adding everything at once to prevent the cottage cheese from becoming trapped underneath the blades of your blender.

Add cheese after removing the blade from the food processor (or placing the mixture in a basin). Mix thoroughly.

If you don't want the extra spice, omit this step and top the chicken with a bit of black pepper and chili pepper.

Add spinach leaves to the chicken's surface.

On top of the spinach, sprinkle the cottage cheese mixture. Make it a thick coating because you'll lose some of it while cooking.

Roll your chicken up gently. While you want to ensure they are tightly sealed, you don't wish the cottage cheese mixture to spill out the sides. The goal is to be tough but kind.

I am showing you this step because it is an optional one. The egg is helpful for egg-brushing. Egg helps the breadcrumbs adhere. While some prefer to coat chicken rolls with water or milk, I usually use an egg.

It's time to break the meat! Although you could use anything you choose, I use my homemade wheat breadcrumbs. I like to place them in the bowl of breadcrumbs, gently roll them, and then sprinkle the breadcrumbs over the chicken to reduce the quantity of stuffing that "escapes.

Cook the chicken roll-ups until they reach a temperature of 165 oF inside. Set the oven to 350° and cook for 20 minutes. Cook at 375° for 20 minutes using an air fryer or Ninja Foodi.

Serve with additional hot sauce or on its own!

Steak Fajita Bowl

Prep Time 10 Minutes

Cook Time 10 Minutes

Total Time 20 Minutes

SERVINGS 4

Equipment
- Instant Pot 6 qt
- Kitchen Knife
- Cutting Board

Ingredients
- 1 tsp olive oil
- 2 tbsp low sodium
- 1 ½ tbsp lime juice, about 1 lime worth
- 1 tbsp garlic minced
- 1 Pound flat iron, but any thin steak will work (slice against the grain)
- 2 bell peppers sliced
- 1 onion large, sliced
- 1 cup quinoa
- ½ cup beef broth low sodium
- Fajita Seasoning:
- 1 tsp cumin
- 1 tbsp chili powder
- 1 tsp paprika
- Optional Toppings:
- tomatoes
- jalapeños
- cilantro

- lime
- avocado
- black beans canned
- corn kernels

Instructions

Instant Pot:

Sauté is selected on the Instant Pot. The sauté mode can be changed to "high" by pressing the "adjust" button. Add the oil once the Instant Pot insert has heated up.

To prepare the dish, kindly add onions, bell peppers, and garlic to the Instant Pot. The vegetables should be sautéed until just barely browned.

The meat, fajita seasonings, lime juice, and liquid Aminos should then be added. Assemble the fajitas and heat the heart for 2–3 minutes or until it is browned.

Switch off the pressure cooker. To create a place for the quinoa, move the fajitas to one side of the Instant Pot. To the empty area, add the quinoa. Do not stir when you pour the beef stock over the quinoa.

Turn the pressure valve to sealing before closing the lid. Cook for two minutes at high pressure using the manual setting. Allow natural pressure relief to occur.

To assemble your fajita bowl, remove the lid. Add any desired toppings as a garnish.

Stove: On your hob, preheat a large skillet. Once the pan is hot, add the oil. To get burn marks, add the steak and bell. Please add peppers, onions, and garlic to the pan. And sauté them—3 to 5 minutes.

Heat setting to medium or low. Lime juice, amino, and fajita seasoning should all be added. After combining:

Push the pan's side.

Fill the space with beef broth, then add the quinoa.

Keep still.

When the quinoa is finished and just beginning to turn translucent, cover the skillet and cook for 15-20 minutes. Take the lid off and allow any extra liquid to cook out.

After putting the bowls together, turn off the stove and serve.

Slow Cooker: Combine all the ingredients for the fajitas in the slow cooker insert, excluding the quinoa and broth.

Place the quinoa in the space left by the fajitas. Do not mix when you pour the beef stock over the quinoa. However, there isn't enough liquid. As the beef cooks, the liquid will be produced.

Cook the slow cooker with the lid on for two hours on high heat or four hours on low heat.

After assembling the bowls and serving, turn off the slow cooker.

Black Bean Brownies with Coconut

Prep Time 10 Minutes

Cook Time 30 Minutes

Total Time 40 Minutes

Serving 16

Equipment

- Food processor
- Baking Dish
- Vitamix Blender

Ingredients

- 15-ounce black beans rinsed and drained
- 2 tbsp cocoa powder
- 1/2 cup oats gluten-free if needed
- 1/2 cup honey
- 1 tsp Stevia Sweetleaf Coconut flavored
- 1 cup coconut unsweetened shredded
- 1/4 cup coconut oil
- 1 tbsp vanilla
- 1 tsp almond extract
- 1/2 tsp baking powder
- 10 Ounces dark chocolate chips

Instructions

Turn the oven on to 350 degrees.

To make beans very smooth, process them in a food processor. I put them in a bowl and used a fork to crush the remaining portions after using my Vitamix to puree them to the extent I could on high.

Add the remaining ingredients to the bowl, excluding the chocolate chips.

Mix until uniform.

Add chocolate chips and mix.

Put the batter in a buttered 8-inch square pan; if desired, top with coconut.

A knife put into the center should come clean after 25 to 30 minutes of baking at 350 degrees (melted chocolate chips excluded).

After cooling it to room temperature, put it in the fridge.

Store your brownies in an airtight container after dividing them into 16 portions.

PowerPoints 12 | 10 Blue Plan Points | 11 Green Plan Points | 10 Purple Plan

Healthy Bang Bang Shrimp Pasta

Prep Time 10 Minutes

Cook Time 20 Minutes

Total Time 30 Minutes

Serving Size: 6

Equipment
- Instant Pot 6 qt
- Kitchen Knife
- Cutting Board

Ingredients
- 13 oz whole wheat pasta spaghetti noodles, dry
- 1 lb shrimp jumbo, raw and FROZEN, peeled & deveined
- 4 cups water
- 3 tsp garlic minced
- 1 tsp coconut oil
- 1/4 cup honey
- 1/4 cup Fresno peppers diced
- 1 lime juiced
- 1/4 tsp pepper
- 1 tbsp vinegar rice
- 1 1/2 cups Greek yogurt plain, 2%
- 1 tbsp sriracha or other hot sauce
- 1/2 cup green onions

Instructions

the Instant Pot to the sauté setting. Add the coconut oil, then let it heat up and melt.

The Fresno peppers and garlic are added next. Saute until aromatic for around 30 seconds.

Place the half-broken spaghetti noodles in the Instant Pot. Over the noodles, pour the water.

On top of the noodles, mix in the frozen prawns, pepper, rice vinegar, honey, and lime. Turn the pressure valve to sealing before closing the lid.

Cook for 3 minutes under high pressure using the manual setting. Utilize a controlled rapid-release technique to release the tension. Use a tool to open and close the pressure valve to reduce the stress released at once. By doing this, the liquid will not stumble.

By doing this, the liquid won't spit out the top.

Greek yogurt, Sriracha, and green onions should all be combined. Serve while heated.

Cook the spaghetti noodles on the hob following the package instructions. Rinse in cold water after draining.

Heat the coconut oil in a skillet over a medium-high flame. Sauté the Fresno peppers and garlic. To the skillet, add the prawns, lime juice, and pepper. Once everything is combined, simmer it for 2-3 minutes to defrost the prawns.

Take off the lid. Add the rice vinegar, honey, and Sriracha together. Cook the prawns for 2-3 minutes or until pink and opaque.

Cut the heat off. Noodles should be added to the prawns in the pan. Greek yogurt and green onions should be combined. Add a garnish and serve hot.

Greek yogurt and green onions are not included in this recipe. Slow cooker: Combine all the ingredients in the slow cooker insert.

The slow cooker's lid should be added. Cook for 2 1/2 hours on low heat or 1 1/2 hours on high heat.

Greek yogurt and green onions are added after the cover has been removed. Serve.

PowerPoints 9 | 9 Blue Plan Points | 10 Green plan Points | 3 Purple Plan Points

Rotisserie Chicken Soup

Prep Time 10 Minutes

Cook Time 25 Minutes

Total Time 35 Minutes

Serving 4

Equipment
- Instant Pot 6 qt
- Crockpot
- Le Creuset Cast Iron Pot

Ingredients
- 1 chicken rotisserie
- 64 Ounces chicken stock low sodium, or if you're fancy, make your own 64 oz.
- 2 cups zucchini diced small
- 1 cup carrots chopped small
- 1 tsp pepper
- 1/2 cup brown rice (dry for IP, cooked for stovetop or Crockpot)
- 1.5 cups salsa

Instructions
Instant Pot:

Cut the rotisserie chicken's meat into bite-sized pieces after removing it from the bird.

To the Instant Pot, add the meat, bones, and skin. To simplify removing the bones and skin afterward, I placed them all on one side of the Instant Pot.

The remaining ingredients should be added to the Instant Pot. Turn the pressure valve to sealing before closing the lid. When preparing rice in the Instant Pot, remember to use dry rice.

Cook for 25 minutes under high pressure on the soup setting. Let the pressure naturally release after the Instant Pot has finished cooking, or you can release the stress by turning the valve slightly, then shutting it again. This will reduce the pressure gradually and stop the soup from bursting through the valve.

When serving the soup, take the bone and skin out. Add diced avocado, cilantro, tortilla strips, and cheese as a garnish.

Stove Top:

Add the salsa and chicken stock to a pot on low heat.

Cook the carrots and zucchini for 5–10 minutes in 1 tablespoon of olive oil.

After that, remove the chicken from the bone. Before adding everything to the saucepan, I laid everything on a cutting board and divided the meat into smaller pieces. Drumsticks, wings, bones, and skin are all added to the cauldron. Do not omit that step, please. It significantly increases moisture and, most importantly, flavor. This bone broth will taste better and offer more significant health benefits. Win-win!

When the vegetables are finished cooking, add the pepper.

Put the rice in. Here, cooked rice is required.!

Simmer (slow boil) on the burner for a full hour. Or two. Maybe three.

Use tongs to remove the skin and bones before eating. I start by adding everything to the bowl except for the broth. Then I put cheese on top. I top the cheese with the broth after it has had time to melt.

Add flour tortilla strips, diced avocado, or both as a garnish!

Slow cooker:

Cut the rotisserie chicken's meat into bite-sized pieces after removing it from the bird.

To the slow cooker, add the meat, bones, and skin. To simplify removing the bones and skin afterward, I put them all in one size of the slow cooker.

The remaining ingredients should be added to the slow cooker. Here, cooked rice is also acceptable.

Put the slow cooker's lid on. Cook the soup for 4-6 hours on low heat or 2-3 hours on high heat.

Remove the skin and bone from the soup before serving it when it's time to dine. Add diced avocado, cilantro, tortilla strips, and cheese as a garnish.

PowerPoints 3 | 3 Blue Plan Point | 5 Green Plan Points | 0 Purple Plan Points

Weight Watchers Goulash

Prep Time 5 Minutes

Cook Time 10 Minutes

Total Time 15 Minutes

Serving 6

Equipment
- Instant Pot 6 qt
- Food processor
- Sealing Rings

Ingredients
- 1 lb ground turkey fat-free
- 1 tbsp garlic minced
- 2 ½ tbsp Italian seasoning
- ½ cup minced onion
- 2 bay leaves take these out after cooking
- 1 cup chopped zucchini
- 1 cup bell peppers chopped
- 14 Ounces crushed tomatoes or a jar of pasta sauce. If using a jar of sauce, omit the spices below.
- 1 cup whole wheat pasta elbow, dry

Instructions
Instant Pot Directions

Spray some oil in your Instant Pot and select Sauté.

Take a spatula and separate the ground turkey into pieces.

Cook till brown and crumbled.

Add bay leaves, onions, garlic, and Italian spice to the pot. Mix thoroughly.

14 ounces of water, and the chopped zucchini, bell peppers, and tomatoes are added.

Add your whole-wheat noodles and stir.

Lock the lid in Place, then turn the valve sealing. Choose Pressure Cooker and enter 3 Minutes as the time.

Quickly release the pressure and remove the lid after the cooking time has passed.

To uniformly combine the ingredients in the pot, stir. If preferred, sprinkle some parmesan cheese on top before serving.

Stovetop Directions

Cook your turkey to an internal temperature of 165°F in a skillet over medium-high heat.

Boil your noodles until they are about Cook It is recommended to cook the pasta al dente, as it will continue to cook further in the sauce. sauces) while your meat is browning.

Stir well after adding the noodles, zucchini, tomatoes, bell peppers, and spices to your turkey.

Ten minutes should be enough time for the vegetables to soften.

If preferred, sprinkle parmesan cheese on top and serve warm.

PowerPoints 2 | 1 Blue Plan Point | 2 Green Plan Points| 0 Purple Plan Points

Breakfast Fajitas

Prep Time 10 Minutes

Cook Time 2 Minutes

Total Time 12 Minutes

Serving 2

Ingredients
- 1 tbsp. olive oil for sautéing
- ½ cup sliced onion
- 1 ½ cup bell peppers sliced
- 4 eggs
- ½ tsp garlic minced
- ½ tsp optional
- Salt and pepper to taste and garnish with cilantro, limes, and avocado

Instructions
Instant Pot

Olive oil should be added, and the Instant Pot should be set to sauté. Bell peppers, garlic, onions, and vegetable seasoning are optional additions. Once the ingredients are aromatic, sauté for about 4 minutes.

Bell peppers and onions should be moved to a round oven-safe pan that will fit inside the Instant Pot once the device has been turned off. Any oven-safe dish would work, but I used a 2-quart soufflé pan.

Four eggs should be gently cracked, and the yolks left whole before being placed on top of the peppers. Wrap with foil. To raise and lower the dish from the Instant Pot, you can create a sling out of a vast sheet of foil that has been folded into thirds.

One cup of water and a trivet should be added to the Instant Pot insert. Put the covered dish on top of the trivet by gently lowering it. Set the pressure valve to seal and lock the lid into position.

Cook for 2 minutes with a fast release under high pressure.

Take the dish out of the pressure cooker. Avocados, cilantro, salt, pepper, and thinly sliced limes can be added as garnishes. I like to serve this with a side of whole-wheat toast!

Heat the olive oil in a skillet over high heat on a hob. Garlic, onions, bell peppers, and vegetable seasoning (optional) should be sautéed for 1-2 minutes after the oil is hot.

Over the vegetables, gently break the eggs. Lower the heat setting to medium.

Cover the pan and simmer for around 1-2 minutes when the egg whites are no longer transparent.

Serve the food immediately, garnished with avocado, limes, and cilantro after taking the skillet off the heat. I like to serve this with a side of whole-wheat toast!

Oven

Set the range to 400 degrees Fahrenheit.

Layer the onions, bell peppers, garlic, olive oil, and vegetable spice (optional) on a baking sheet after tossing them in the mixture.

Over the vegetables, gently break the eggs. Depending on how tender you prefer your eggs, please Place them in the oven and bake for 12 to 15 minutes.

After removing from the oven, serve right away. Add cilantro, limes, and avocado slices on top.

PowerPoints 2, 2 Blue Plan Points, 6 Green Plan Points, 2 Purple Plan Point

Mocha Coffee Creamer with Almond Milk

Prep Time 10 Minutes

Cook Time 2Minutes

Total Time 12 Minutes

Serving 17

Equipment
- Le Creuset Cast Iron Pot
- Whisk
- Egg Bite Molds

Ingredients
- 1 can coconut milk total fat, unsweetened
- 3 tbsp almond milk unsweetened, chocolate if you'd like
- 2 tbsp coconut crystals
- 2 tsp cocoa powder
- 1 tsp vanilla extract

Instructions
A small pot should be filled with coconut milk, almond milk, cocoa powder, coconut crystals, and vanilla.

Cocoa powder and coconut crystals should dissolve while whisking over low heat.

Remove the pan from the heat after turning off the hob. After letting the creamer cool naturally for 20 minutes, put it to an airtight glass container before cooling it down. Additionally, this recipe can be frozen in ice cube trays or egg bite molds.

For 5-7 days in the fridge or three months in the freezer.

Instant Pot Vegan Minestrone Soup

Prep Time 10 Minutes

Cook Time 4 Minutes

Total Time 14 Minutes

Serving 8

Equipment
- Instant Pot 6 qt
- Kitchen Knife
- Cutting Board

Ingredients
- 1 cup red onion diced
- 2 ½ cups celery diced
- 2 ½ cups carrots peeled and sliced
- 2 cups diced zucchini
- 1 cup spinach
- 1 cup whole wheat pasta dry (elbows will triple in size for this recipe)
- ½ cup kidney beans (canned)
- ½ cup white beans (canned)
- 1 can diced tomatoes low sodium
- 64 Ounces low sodium vegetable broth
- 1 tbsp oregano
- ½ tsp salt
- 4 tsp basil
- 2 tsp sage
- 4 tsp garlic fresh, minced
- 2 tsp parsley
- 2 bay leaves

Instructions
Instant Pot

Slice the zucchini, onions, celery, and carrots. If you'd like, you can cut the spinach.

Spray the bottom of the pot with cooking spray before adding every vegetable but spinach to your pressure cooker and setting it to sauté.

Add your spices to the pot after a few minutes of sautéing, excluding the bay leaves. Remember that the vegetables won't complete cooking right away. Stir to distribute the seasoning evenly.

Turn off the heat and add the pasta, bay leaves, drained beans, chopped tomatoes, and vegetable broth once your spices and vegetables smell fragrant.

Set the valve to sealing and close the lid. Set your pressure cooker for 4 minutes if necessary and press "start."

Carefully open the sealing vent and let the pressure out once the timer goes off and your soup is ready.

Add the spinach after lifting the cover. For 2-3 minutes, stir the soup and cover once more.

Shut the cover and stir your soup. Pull out the bay leaves by locating them. Enjoy!

Stovetop

Cut zucchini, onions, celery, and carrots into dice. If you'd like, you can cut the spinach.

Spray the bottom of a large pot that will be used to cook soup on medium-high on the stove. It should have enough space to accommodate 64 ounces of broth and vegetables—Sauté all vegetables, spinach excluded.

Add your spices to the pot after a few minutes of sautéing, omitting the bay leaves.

Add pasta, rinsed beans, diced tomatoes, and vegetable broth once your spices smell fragrant. The bay leaves should be removed from the soup after it has finished cooking and before you consume it.

Bring your soup to a simmer (where little bubbles form from the bottom and periodically burst to the top) and boil until the pasta is al dente. Check the pasta's label for the cooking time, which should be around 10 minutes.

Remove the bay leaves from the saucepan after the noodles are cooked, then add the spinach and toss it into the broth. Serve after letting it sit and wilt for a few minutes.

Coffee Creamer & Vanilla Coffee Creamer

Prep Time 5 Minutes

Cook Time 5 Minutes

Total Time 10 Minutes

Serving 17

Equipment
- Le Creuset Cast Iron Pot
- Glass Milk Bottles

Ingredients
- 1 can coconut milk total fat, unsweetened
- 3 tbsp almond milk unsweetened
- 2 tbsp coconut crystals, also called coconut sugar
- 1 tbsp vanilla extract

Instructions
Add coconut milk, almond milk, coconut crystals, and vanilla essence to a small saucepan. Combine by whisking.

Stirring constantly, heat on low until crystals are well incorporated with the other ingredients.

Before putting the food in the refrigerator, please turn off the heat and let it cool for 20 minutes.

5-7 days in the refrigerator, or freeze.

PowerPoints 3, 3 Blue Plan Points | 3 Green Plan Points | 3 Purple Plan Points

Cilantro Lime Chicken Drumsticks

Prep Time 5 Minutes

Cook Time 15 Minutes

Total Time 20 Minutes

Serving 3

Equipment
- Instant Pot 6 qt
- Olive Oil Spray
- Sealing Rings

Ingredients
- 1 tbsp olive oil
- 6 drumsticks
- 4 cloves minced garlic
- 1 tsp crushed red peppers
- 1 tsp cayenne pepper
- juice from 1 lime
- 2 tbsp chopped cilantro
- 1/2 cup chicken broth Low Sodium

Instructions
Instant Pot Instructions

Press Saute after adding the olive oil to the Instant Pot. The chicken drumsticks should be added once the oil is heated. The drumsticks should be seasoned with minced garlic, crushed red pepper, and cayenne pepper. Each side for 2 minutes to brown.

Add lime juice, cilantro, and chicken stock to the Instant Pot. Turn the pressure valve to Seal after locking the lid into position.

Cook for 9 minutes at high pressure.

Allow the pressure to release once the cooking is done naturally.

Place the drumsticks on a baking sheet. Broil for 3 to 5 minutes until the surface turns golden brown. Serve immediately after adding fresh cilantro.

Oven Guidelines

Skip the chicken broth if you're baking the chicken drumsticks.

Turn on the 375-degree oven. Put the chicken, cilantro, lime juice, crushed red peppers, cayenne pepper, and garlic in a zip-top bag. The recipe might need to be divided between two bags.

Shake the bags to evenly coat the drumsticks with the cilantro-lime marinade.

Oil a 9x13 pan very lightly. On your pan, arrange the drumsticks in a single layer. Sprinkle the chicken with any additional seasonings that are still in the bag. You may need a larger pan depending on how many drumsticks you're cooking.

After 30 minutes of baking, delicately turn the drumsticks using tongs. Bake for 30 minutes or until a meat thermometer registers 165 degrees within the dish.

PowerPoints 7, 6 Blue Points | 6 Green Points | 6 Purple Points.

Baked Oatmeal | Apple Cinnamon

Prep Time 2 Minutes

Cook Time 10 Minutes

Total Time 12 Minutes

Serving 1

Equipment
- Instant Pot 6 qt
- Sealing Rings
- Kitchen Knife

Ingredients
- ½ cup oats I prefer rolled oats for this recipe.
- 1/3 cup almond milk or coconut
- ¼ tsp baking powder
- ¼ tsp cinnamon
- ½ tsp vanilla
- 1 tsp maple syrup (optional)
- 1 egg
- ¼ cup diced apples, optional
- coconut oil spray optional

Instructions
Get your pot ready: Set the trivet at the bottom of the saucepan and add 2 cups of water. Spray oil into your large ramekins, coffee mugs, and Mason jars.

Add all of your components, including the dry and liquid ones: Thoroughly combine and mix all the ingredients with a spoon. Alternatively, you can combine all the ingredients in a bowl and spoon the oat mixture into the jars one at a time.

Muesli cups should be carefully placed in the saucepan so they don't topple.

Close and lock the cover, then set the cooking timer for 10 minutes on high pressure. Release the stress quickly after the cooking time is over. After that, remove the top and carefully lift the muesli cups.

Enjoy: Serve warm or take it with you as you leave the house. Add more syrup, sliced bananas, other fruits like berries or peanut butter, and your favorite toppings.

To prepare several servings

In individual mugs, 1-4 servings can be heated for 10 minutes. Cook up to 8 servings of muesli for 20 minutes if you're cooking a dish with more than one serving.

PowerPoints 3 | 4 Blue Plan Points, 6 Green Plan Points, 0 Purple Points. If using maple syrup 4 Points on the 2023 Plan | 5 Blue Plan Points, 7 Green Plan Points, 1 Purple Plan Point.

Cloud Bread with Cream Cheese

Prep Time 10 Minutes

Cook Time 25 Minutes

Total Time 35 Minutes

Serving 2

Equipment
- Silpat Mat
- hand mixer

Ingredients
- 3 eggs at room temperature and separated
- 3 tbsp light cream cheese at room temperature
- ¼ tsp baking powder

Instructions
Set the oven to 300 °F. Use parchment paper or a Silpat mat to cover a cookie sheet.

Combine cream cheese and egg yolks; reserve the egg whites for another use. Make sure all of the cream cheese clumps are removed.

Add baking powder and egg whites to a second bowl until fluffy, whip. Ensure that the firmness of the egg whites is consistent throughout the entire dish.

The whites and yolks should be combined gently. I blend the ingredients with a large whisk, ensuring not to overmix. Thus, the cloud bread will remain fluffy.

To allow for expansion:

To drop the batter onto the surface, use a cookie scoop. Covered baking sheet, spacing it about 2 inches apart.

Place the cookie sheet in the oven and bake it for the recommended time. Twenty-five minutes or until golden brown.

Before putting the cloud bread in an airtight container in the refrigerator, move it to a cooling rack.

Spring Roll Salad

Prep Time 25 Minutes

Cook Time 0 Minutes

Total Time 25 Minutes

Serving Size 2

Equipment
- Mixing Bowls
- Kitchen Knife
- Cutting Board

Ingredients
- Salad Ingredients
- 4 cups Lettuce
- 1 cup Red bell pepper diced
- 1 cup Cucumber diced
- 1 cup Carrots shredded
- 1/2 cup Purple cabbage shredded
- 8 leaves Fresh basil
- 1 cube Tofu cubed
- 1 cake of Brown rice ramen cooked
- 1/4 cup Edamame shelled
- 3 stalks Green onions thinly sliced

Dressing Ingredients

- 1/4 cup
- 1/8 cup Peanut butter creamy
- 1/2 tsp Maple syrup
- 1 1/2 tsp Sriracha or chili paste
- 1 1/2 tsp Roasted sesame oil

Instructions

Organize your workspace and place a chopping board, a good knife, and a big bowl there.

As directed on the package, prepare the noodles. I like to sprinkle some roasted sesame oil on the ramen after it has finished cooking to prevent sticking. Also significant is the flavor.

It would help if you began by chopping and slicing your vegetables while the ramen cooks.

Combine the salad dressing ingredients in a mason jar or small bowl.

Next, add the cooked ramen and vegetables to your salad dish. The salad dressing is then added to your bowl. According to your preferences, season the salad, and It's best to store any extra sauce in a container that seals tightly.

Serve the salad right away after tossing the ingredients together until well combined. PowerPoints 0

Weight Watchers Egg Bites

Prep Time 5 Minutes

Cook Time 8 Minutes

Total Time 13 Minutes

Serving 7

Equipment

- Instant Pot 6 qt
- Egg Bite Molds
- Sealing Rings

Ingredients

- 6 eggs
- 1 cup cheddar cheese shredded, fat-free (optional)
- ¾ cup cottage cheese fat-free
- ¾ cup Greek yogurt fat-free, plain
- ½ cup sun-dried tomatoes in water
- ¼ cup chopped basil

Instructions

Instant Pot

Combine the eggs, cheddar cheese, fat-free cottage cheese, and fat-free Greek yogurt in a Blend the ingredients in a blender on high speed for 30 seconds or until smooth. Thoroughly combined and foamy.

Two silicone egg molds should be sprayed with cooking before being filled with a sun-dried tomato and some basil. Each cup should be roughly 3/4 full of the egg mixture. The molds should be tightly covered with aluminum foil.

Place a trivet in the bottom of your Instant Pot after adding 1 cup of water. Place the trivet on top of your molds.

Lock the lid, then turn the pressure release valve to the sealing position. Set the timer for 8 minutes and choose Pressure Cook (high).

After the cooking period is through, let the pressure naturally release. Remove the cover after the pressure valve releases, then carefully remove the aluminum foil and molds. Before removing the egg bites from the refrigerator or counter, let them cool. For up to a week, keep egg bites in the fridge.

When you're ready to consume them,30 to 45 seconds in the microwave should be sufficient.

Oven

Set the oven to 375°F.

Combine the eggs, cheddar cheese, fat-free cottage cheese, and fat-free Greek yogurt in a blender. Blend on high for 30 seconds or until thoroughly combined and foamy.

Add sun-dried tomato and some basil to the bottom of each cup. Spray two silicone egg molds or a cupcake pan with cooking spray. Each cup should be roughly 3/4 full of the egg mixture.

Bake for 20 minutes or until frothy and gently browned. The egg bites will rise during cooking, but they will sink after cooling.

Before taking out the egg bites:

Let them cool.

For up to a week, keep egg bites in the refrigerator.

Warm them in the microwave for 30 to 45 seconds when you are prepared to consume them.

PowerPoints 0, 3 Blue Plan Points | 5 Green Plan Points | 2 Purple Plan Points

Swedish Meatballs

Prep Time 25 Minutes

Cook Time 5 Minutes

Total Time 30 Minutes

Serving 4

Equipment
- Instant Pot 6 qt
- Sealing Rings
- Mixing Bowls

Ingredients
- 1 Pound ground turkey
- 1 tsp paprika
- 1 tsp onion powder chopped
- 1 tsp garlic powder
- ½ tsp pepper
- 1 tsp allspice
- 1 ½ cups low-sodium chicken broth
- 1 tbsp low sodium soy sauce
- 1 tbsp mustard
- ¾ cup plain Greek yogurt fat-free
- 1/4 cup fresh parsley chopped
- Optional, not included in the points count
- 2 tbsp parmesan cheese
- 1/4 tsp salt and pepper

Instructions

Combine ground turkey, paprika, onion, garlic, pepper, and allspice in a medium-sized bowl. Combine with your hands until thoroughly combined, then shape into 16 meatballs of the same size.

Spray some olive oil into your Instant Pot and set it to sauté. Give your meatballs a 30-second sear on each side—one layer at a time, brown in small amounts.

Scrape any turkey bits from the pot's bottom. Mix the ingredients using a spatula or wooden spoon before pouring the liquid. Add mustard and low-sodium soy sauce.

Place the pressure valve in the sealing position, then close and lock the lid. Set the pressure in your pot. Cook for 5 minutes on high.

Quickly release the pressure and remove the lid after the cooking period.

Your meatballs can now be removed and placed aside. Mix well before adding Greek yogurt and parsley to the hot saucepan. Add some cornflour to your gravy and stir well if it looks to be too thin.

Re-add the cooked meatballs to the cooking vessel. Serve the meatballs warm after stirring gently until they are coated evenly. Add fresh Parmesan on top, if preferred.

A different method for cooking meatballs is to roll and freeze them for 30 minutes. Skip the second step in the instructions and pressure cook for 7 minutes rather than 5.

PowerPoints 0, 2 Blue Plan Points | 3 Green Plan Points | 2 Purple Plan Points.

Brown Rice Risotto with Mushrooms

Prep Time 5 Minutes

Cook Time 35 Minutes

Total Time 40 Minutes

Serving 12

Equipment
- Instant Pot 6 qt
- Sealing Rings
- Kitchen Knife

Ingredients
- 2 tbsp olive oil
- 1 shallot diced
- 1 lb mushrooms sliced. I used a gourmet blend, but baby Bellas work as well
- 1 cup chopped asparagus
- 1 lb chicken thighs frozen, boneless, skinless
- ½ tsp pepper
- 1 ½ cups brown rice short grain
- 5 cups chicken broth low sodium
- 1/4 cup parmesan cheese shredded

- Optional: salt to taste

Instructions

Add olive oil to the bottom of your Instant Pot and set it to sauté. Add the chopped shallots, mushrooms, and asparagus once the oil is hot. Cook the shallots until they are aromatic and transparent, stirring regularly. Put the vegetables on a platter and reserve.

Add the frozen chicken breast to the hot Instant Pot and fry it all over. Add rice, broth, and black pepper after turning the Instant Pot off.

Lock the lid in Place, then turn the sealing pressure valve. Choose Pressure Using the high setting, cook for 25 minutes.

Let the pressure freely relax when the cooking period has ended. Remove the cover after the pressure valve has depressed and shred the chicken thighs with two forks. The use of a stand mixer can facilitate shredding.

Stir in the sautéed shallots, mushrooms, asparagus, and parmesan cheese after setting the Instant Pot to sauté. Cook the cheese for 2 to 3 minutes or until it melts. Serve right away after removing from heat. Refer to the notes and suggestions section for advice on freezing and reheating meals.

Banana Pancakes

Prep Time 3 Minutes

Cook Time 3 Minutes

Total Time 6 Minutes

Serving 1

Equipment
- Mixing Bowls
- Whisk
- Enameled Cast Iron Pan

Ingredients
- 1 banana ripe
- 1 egg

Instructions

Spray your pan liberally, then set it over medium heat.

Put your banana in a basin and mash it with a fork or potato masher until completely smooth.

Bananas should be thoroughly mixed with the egg when it has been added.

Pour your batter into a skillet that has been preheated, and then leave it alone to cook for 3–4 minutes or until the edges start to dry up. Flip your pancake carefully, then cook another 2-3 minutes. Place your preferred toppings on your pancake after transferring it to a platter. I enjoy both maple syrup and peanut butter.

Weight Watchers Breakfast Fried Rice

Prep Time 15 Minutes

Cook Time 25 Minutes

Total Time 40 Minutes

Serving 6

Equipment
- Kitchen Knife
- Measuring Cups
- Coconut Aminos

Ingredients
- ¼ cup of low-sodium tamari or soy sauce
- ¼ tsp dry mustard
- ½ cup red onion diced
- 1 tbsp garlic minced
- 1 cup bell pepper diced
- 2 links of chicken sausage diced. I use Adelle's' all-natural chicken and apple sausage
- 1 cup peas & carrots frozen
- 2 eggs scrambled
- 4 slices of turkey bacon cooked and cut into bite-sized pieces
- 3 cups brown rice cooked and cooled, cook the day before and store in the refrigerator
- optional: low-sodium ham

Instructions
Combine mustard and soy sauce or coconut aminos Place aside.

In a big skillet or wok, heat one tablespoon of oil, then add

Sausage, bell pepper, onions, and garlic can all be added now, along with other ingredients.

3- to 5-minute sauté.

Add carrots, peas, and bacon. When cooking eggs in a pan, shift the food to one side before cracking and scrambling the eggs.

the pan with your cooked rice,

The mixture of sauce and rice should be poured over and gently mixed.

If you didn't cook the eggs in the pan, gently stir them now. Cook until well heated.

PowerPoints 7 | 9 Blue Points | 10 Green Points | 5 Purple Points

Healthy Drunken Noodles

Prep Time 20 Minutes

Cook Time 6 Minutes

Total Time 26 Minutes

Serving 4

Equipment
- Instant Pot 6 qt
- Kitchen Knife
- Cutting Board

Ingredients
- 1 Pounds chicken breast cut into thin ½ -inch strips
- 2 carrots peeled and cut into strips, about 2C
- 1 bell pepper red, chopped
- 2 cups mushrooms
- 3 cups bok choy chopped
- 4 tsp garlic minced
- 2 dried chili pods and Thai chilies are best! or you can substitute with 1 tsp crushed red peppers
- 2 cups whole wheat pasta dry
- ½ cup low sodium soy sauce I prefer coconut aminos, but you can also use low sodium tamari.
- 1 tbsp honey
- 2 cups water
- ½ cup scallions diced
- ½ cup basil fresh, chopped

Instructions
Instant Pot

Cut your chicken into thin (12 inch) strips.

Spray a thin layer of oil inside the pot.

Cut your carrots into small strips after peeling them. Chop bok choy, mushrooms, and bell peppers. To ensure consistent cooking, cut all your vegetables roughly the same size.

Sauté the garlic, Thai chili pods, mushrooms, and chicken for two to three minutes after the oil is hot. To prevent the chicken from sticking together, stir thoroughly.

Add the noodles, water, honey, and soy sauce.

Do not stir after adding the chicken's bok choy, bell peppers, and carrots.

Turn the pressure valve to sealing before closing the lid—3 minutes of high-pressure cooking.

Quickly release the pressure after the timer expires.

Dispense and savour! Please keep it in the refrigerator in an airtight container for Dispense and savor! For 3–4 days, keep in the fridge in an airtight container.

Spray a large skillet lightly.

Over high heat, sauté the chicken, mushrooms, red chili pods, garlic, and for about 2 minutes.

Add carrots, bell pepper, and bok choy to the skillet. Sauté the bok choy until it wilts.

Add the noodles, water, honey, and soy sauce. Boil the liquid, cover it, and heat it to medium or low.

Until the pasta is cooked, let the spaghetti simmer for 12 to 15 minutes while stirring occasionally.

Add the basil and scallions after removing the lid.

Dispense and savour! Keep in the refrigerator in an airtight container for Dispense and savour! For 3–4 days, keep in the fridge in an airtight container.

Crockpot: Fill the slow cooker with the chicken, chili flakes, garlic, soy sauce, water, and honey. So that the chicken is covered, combine everything.

On top of the chicken, arrange the carrots, bell peppers, mushrooms, and bok choy.

Put a lid on the slow cooker.

Cook the chicken entirely for two to three hours on low heat. During the final 15 minutes of cooking, add the noodles.

Add the basil and scallions after.

Dispense and savour! Keep in the refrigerator in an airtight container for Dispense and savour! Keep in an airtight container in the fridge for 3 to 4 days.

PowerPoints 7, 4 Blue Points | 6 Green Points | 1 Purple Point |

Instant Pot Lentil Tacos

Prep Time 10 Minutes

Cook Time 12 Minutes

Resting Time 5 Minutes

Total Time 22 Minutes

Serving 4

Equipment
- Instant Pot 6 qt

Ingredients
- 1 cup French lentils
- ¼ cup corn kernels
- ¼ cup black beans canned
- 1 cup diced tomatoes with green chilies in liquid
- ½ cup tomato sauce low sodium
- 2 cups vegetable broth, low sodium, or water | none if lentils are pre-cooked
- 1 tbsp garlic minced
- 2 stalks of celery chopped
- 1 tsp taco seasoning

Instructions

Stir everything well in your Instant Pot after adding all the ingredients.

Choose "Soup/Chilli" as the setting and give it 12 minutes. (If the lentils have already been cooked, choose 5 Minutes.)

Seal and let the release occur naturally.

Before serving, taste and make any necessary flavor adjustments. Sour cream, cheese, and cilantro garnishes are optional.

PowerPoints 0 | 0 Blue Plan Points | 5 Green Plan Points | | 0 Purple Plan Points

Instant Pot Italian Meatballs

Prep Time 30 Minutes

Cook Time 8 Minutes

Total Time 38 Minutes

Serving 4

Equipment
- Instant Pot 6 qt
- Instant Pot Trivet

Ingredients
- 1 Pound ground beef extra lean
- 1 egg
- ⅓ cup rolled oats
- 2 tbsp Parmesan cheese grated
- 4 cloves garlic minced
- 2 tbsp Italian seasoning
- 1 tsp crushed red pepper flakes

Instructions

Ground beef, eggs, rolled oats, Parmesan cheese, garlic, Italian seasoning, and red pepper flakes should all be thoroughly blended in a large basin.

Make 24 meatballs with a cookie scoop, then roll each into a ball with your hands.

Meatballs should be placed on a cookie sheet and frozen for at least 15 minutes.

Place your trivet in the bottom of the Instant Pot after adding 1/2 cup of water, then wait while the meatballs chill.

Put the trivet on top of the cold meatballs.

Put the pressure valve in the sealing position, and close and lock the lid.

Pressure 8 minutes on high during cooking.

Five minutes should pass naturally before you quickly remove any leftover pressure.

Remove the trivet gently, then disentangle any stalled meatballs. Serve right away or keep in the refrigerator for up to 5 days.

PowerPoints 4 | 4 Blue Plan Points | 4 Green Plan Points | 3 Purple Plan Points

Air Fryer Buffalo Cauliflower from Raw or Frozen

Prep Time 5 Minutes

Cook Time 20 Minutes

Total Time 25 Minutes

Serving 2

Equipment
- Nutritional Yeast
- Ninja Foodi
- Mixing Bowls

Ingredients
- 2 cups cauliflower frozen florets, thawed or raw
- olive oil spray or butter
- ½ cup hot sauce I use Frank's regular hot sauce, not buffalo sauce.
- ¾ cup nutritional yeast or panko breadcrumbs (optional)

Instructions
Instructions for an air fryer

Heat the air fryer to 400 degrees.

2 cups of cauliflower florets should be added to a sizable mixing basin. Cooking spray or melted butter should be used liberally, and the cauliflower should be thoroughly coated. Put some Frank's red hot sauce on.

Toss the cauliflower in the hot sauce until it is evenly coated.

One more time, add nutritional yeast and toss. Crushed crackers or bread crumbs are other options.

Set the air fryer basket's cook timer for 20 minutes and add the cauliflower in a single layer. Don't overcrowd the air fryer because the cauliflower needs room to circulate hot air to cook it. Give your cauliflower a gentle toss every five minutes to encourage equal cooking and browning.

Cooking the cauliflower will take 10 to 15 minutes.

When your cauliflower is ready to eat, it should be well-browned and crispy. Continue cooking in 5-minute intervals if it seems soggy. Your air fryer might take longer or less time because they all produce distinct outcomes.

When the cauliflower is crisp and gently browned, please remove it.

Oven Guidelines

Set the oven to 400 °F.

2 cups of cauliflower should be added to a big bowl. Add your spicy sauce after liberally spraying it with cooking spray and shaking it to ensure it is evenly coated. Stir and toss the cauliflower in the spicy sauce until it is evenly coated, then add the nutritional yeast and mix again.

Place your cauliflower on a covered baking sheet. To prepare, cover a baking sheet with parchment paper. Roast the ingredients for 10-15 minutes. Or until golden and crispy.

PowerPoints 1 | 4 Blue Plan Points | 4 Green Plan Points | 4 Purple Plan Points

Healthy White Chicken Chili

Prep Time 10 Minutes

Cook Time 45 Minutes

Total Time 55 Minutes

Serving 4

Equipment
- Instant Pot 6 qt
- Cutting Board
- Kitchen Knife

Ingredients
- 1.5 – 2 lbs. chicken breast must be frozen to allow time for the beans to cook
- 1 cup white beans dried, washed but not soaked
- 3 green chilis fresh, diced | I used poblano
- 2 jalapeños chopped
- 1 bell pepper red, chopped, about 1 cup
- 1 onion yellow, chopped | about 1/2 cup
- 4 cloves garlic minced
- ½ tbsp cumin
- ½ tbsp chili powder
- ½ tsp pepper
- 2 cups chicken broth
- 1 cup almond milk unsweetened
- ¾ cup Greek yogurt plain, 2%

Instructions
Instant Pot

Everything but the plain Greek yoghurt and the frozen chicken should be placed in the Instant Pot.

Stir the chili briefly to distribute the seasoning evenly.

Place the frozen chicken on top to make shredding the cooked chicken easy.

Turn the pressure valve to sealing before closing the lid. Use the "bean," "manual", or "pressure cook" buttons for cooking the chili under high pressure for 45 minutes. Before doing a fast release, allow the pressure to release naturally for at least 10 minutes.

Reintroduce the chicken to the chili after shredding it.

Set the Instant Pot to the sauté setting. Include the Greek yoghurt. If you'd like the chili to thicken even more, boil it for 10-15 minutes.

Serve after adding cheese, cilantro, and avocado.

Slow Cooker

Place everything in the slow cooker minus the frozen chicken and Greek yoghurt.

Stir the chili briefly to distribute the seasoning evenly.

Place the frozen chicken on top to make shredding the cooked chicken easy.

Put a lid on the slow cooker. Cook for 6 to 8 hours at low heat.

Chicken should be removed, shredded, and then added to the chili.

Include the Greek yoghurt.

Serve after adding cheese, cilantro, and avocado.

Stovetop

Let your beans soak all night.

In a big pot, combine all the ingredients minus the Greek yogurt.

On high heat, bring the chili to a boil; then, put a lid on it and turn the heat down to low.

Stirring as necessary, let the chili simmer for two to three hours or until the beans are soft.

Shred the chicken after removing the lid. Reintroduce the chicken to the chili.

Include the Greek yoghurt. Let the chili boil for an additional period of time until the chili achieves the appropriate thickness.

Serve after adding cheese, cilantro, and avocado.

PowerPoints 0 | 1 Blue Plan Points | 9 Green Plan Points | 1 Purple Plan Point

Vegan Chili

Prep Time 15 Minutes

Cook Time 40 Minutes

Total Time 55 Minutes

Serving 6

Equipment
- Enameled Cast Iron Pan
- Cutting Board
- Kitchen Knife

Ingredients
- 1 pound carrots peeled and chopped into 1/4 inch half moons
- 1 medium red onion diced
- 14 Ounces low sodium black beans undrained
- 14 Ounces of soft sodium kidney beans undrained
- 14 Ounces soft sodium cannellini beans or white beans, undrained
- 14 Ounces of soft sodium pinto beans undrained
- 28 Ounces diced tomatoes
- 3 tbsp chili powder. Skip if you don't like spice
- 1 tbsp cumin
- 1 tsp garlic powder
- ¾ tsp onion powder
- ¼ tsp salt
- ¼ tsp ground black pepper
- ½ cup water or broth

Instructions
Spray olive oil in a big saucepan or Dutch oven and cook the carrots for 5-7 minutes on medium heat.

Saute for 5 minutes after adding the seasonings and diced onions.

Fill the pot with water, beans, and tomatoes. Cook for 30 to 40 minutes or until heated; the flavors are well-balanced.

Add some green onions, diced.

For 4-5 days, keep leftover chili in an airtight jar.

PowerPoints 0

Weight Watchers Beef Gyros In The Instant Pot

Prep Time 5 Minutes

Cook Time 14 Minutes

Total Time 19 Minutes

Serving 6

Equipment
- Instant Pot 6 qt
- Sealing Rings
- Kitchen Knife

Ingredients
- Gyros
- 1 red onion thinly sliced
- 2 Pounds flank steak thinly sliced; I've also used loin flap meat, and it's so easy to slice and cook!
- 3 cloves garlic minced
- 1 tbsp parsley dried
- 1 tbsp lemon juice
- ½ cup beef broth low sodium
- 6 pitas
- Tzatziki Sauce:
- 1 cup plain Greek yogurt
- ½ Cucumber peeled, seeded, shredded
- 1 clove garlic minced
- 2 tbsp fresh dill

Optional Toppings:

- ½ cup diced cucumbers
- ½ cup carrots thinly sliced
- ½ cup diced onions
- ½ cup shredded lettuce
- ½ cup diced tomatoes
- ½ cup feta cheese

Instructions
Instant Pot Directions

Use black pepper and dried parsley to season your flank steak. Slice your steak and red onion thinly. I advise cutting the steak against the grain and not making it thicker than 1/4". Make minced garlic.

Cooking spray your Instant Pot lightly and set it to sauté. When the oil is hot, add the onions, garlic, and sauté for about 3 minutes or until the onions soften. Your sliced steak, beef broth, and lemon juice are then added.

Lock the lid in Place, then turn the sealing pressure valve. Set the cook duration to 9 Minutes and choose Pressure Cook (high pressure).

Combine the Greek yogurt, chopped cucumbers, garlic, and dill in a small bowl while the meat cooks. Until it's time to serve, please keep it in the refrigerator.

Following the end of the cooking period, quickly release the pressure and remove the lid. Serve right away.

Directions for the stove

Use black pepper and dried parsley to season your flank steak. Slice your steak and red onion thinly. I advise cutting the steak against the grain and not making it thicker than 1/4". Make minced garlic.

Heat a skillet to medium-high and coat with cooking spray.

Garlic, onions, and meat should all be added to the pan and sautéed until the onions soften.

Bring the broth and lemon juice to a boil, then lower the heat and simmer for 10 to 15 minutes.

Serve with chosen toppings on top of pita or naan bread.

PowerPoints 6 | 5 Blue Plan Points | 6 Green Plan Points | 5 Purple Plan Points.

Slow Cooker Pizza Stuffed Peppers

Prep Time 10 Minutes

Cook Time 1 hour 5 Minutes

Total Time 1 hour 15 Minutes

Serving 8

Equipment
- Crockpot
- Baking Sheet
- Enameled Cast Iron Pan

Ingredients
- olive oil 1 spray
- 1 Pounds ground turkey sausage Italian
- 1 ½ cups marinara sauce low sugar
- 4 bell peppers halved
- 4 tbsp water
- 1 cup mozzarella cheese

Instructions

Using a slow cooker, make pizza-stuffed peppers

Sausage should be cooked until browned in a big skillet.

Add marinara sauce and stir.

Cook for 5 minutes while covered.

Fill peppers with sausage mixture, then top with remaining sauce.

Put cheese on top.

In the Ninja Foodi/Slow Cooker, arrange the ingredients in an even layer, add the water, and choose the high slow cook mode for 1 hour.

If using the Ninja Foodi, set it to air crisp at 325°. Once it has been an hour, follow the slow cooking of your peppers on high. Keep an eye on them because the cheese will melt, and the peppers will become crunchy in just a few minutes. Feel free to add more if the Minutes aren't crisping up to your pleasure. The cheese and the peppers should not be burned.

If there are any leftovers, place them in an airtight container and refrigerate after allowing them to cool to room temperature.

How to prepare pizza-stuffed peppers in the oven or on the hob

Spray some olive oil in a big skillet and brown the sausage there.

Add marinara sauce and stir.

Cook for 5 minutes with a cover on.

Fill the pepper halves with the sausage. First, mix the ingredients. Afterward, put the peppers into a baking dish. Or on a baking sheet.

If desired, top with cheese or any other preferred pizza elements.

Thirty minutes of cooking at 350.

PowerPoints 3, 3 Blue Plan Points | 4 Green Plan Points | 3 Purple Plan Points

Cauliflower, potato, and leek soup

Prep Time 15 Minutes

Cook Time 4 Minutes

Total Time 19 Minutes

Servings 8

Ingredients
- 1 head of cauliflower
- 2 stalks of leek
- 3 medium potatoes (peeled and cubed)
- 2 cloves of garlic (diced)
- 3 cups broth (I used vegetables)
- Salt & Pepper (just a dash)
- 1/2 cup 0% plain Greek yogurt

Instructions
Wash and split your cauliflower. Peel and dice your potatoes.

Wash leeks (the best manner is to reduce their length cleverly. If you need to wash the insides of the fruits, you can use a knife to open them up. Cube them as you will inexperienced onion.

Dice up garlic, and upload it all in your crock pot.

Pour in broth and upload salt & Pepper.

Let prepare dinner Excessive 3-4 hours or low 7-8 hours.

Using an inversion blender (or normal one) combo soup, upload for your yogurt and blend once more till exceptional and creamy if it's miles too thick; experience unfastened to feature in a bit of water or more excellent broth.

Makes 8 cups (possibly a bit greater or less depending on the size of potatoes and cauliflower)

PersonalPoints 3

Creamy potato & cauliflower cheesy soup

Prep Time 15 Minutes

Cook Time 4 Hrs

Total Time 4 Hrs 15 Minutes

Servings 8

Ingredients

- 4 medium peeled white potatoes
- ½ head of chopped cauliflower
- 1 small chopped onion
- 4 cups of broth (your choice)
- ½ cup milk (I use almond)
- 2/3 cup light-grated mozzarella
- 2 Tbsp aioli sauce (optional)
- 2 Tbsp light cream cheese
- salt/pepper to taste

Instructions

On high for 4 hours or low for 6 hours, cook the potatoes, cauliflower, onion, and broth in the slow cooker.

While the potatoes and cauliflower are cooking in the crock pot, mash them with a hand masher. Stir a few times after adding the sauce, cheese, and milk.

For 10 to 15 minutes, leave the cheese to melt on low. Add shredded cheese and bacon crumbs as a garnish. (Optional; does not count toward point total) per serving of 1 cup, 4sp, or 3pp.

PersonalPoints

4sp or 3pp per serving

Creamy potato and cheese soup

Prep Time 10 Minutes

Cook Time 6 Hrs 30 Minutes

Total Time 6 Hrs 40 Minutes

Servings 10

Ingredients

- 6 medium-sized potatoes (peeled and cut into cubes)
- 1 cup diced onion
- 2 garlic cloves (diced)
- 3 cups chicken broth
- Salt & pepper
- 1 cup almond milk (I use unsweetened original)
- 4 T light cream cheese
- 2/3 cup light shredded cheese

Instructions

Potatoes should be peeled, sliced, and placed in a slow cooker.

Add the chicken broth, onions, garlic, salt, and Pepper to taste. Cook for approximately 6 hours on low. Mash up the potatoes using a hand masher. Add the milk and cheese, stir, and simmer for 20 to 30 minutes to melt the cheese.

Add some cheese and bacon bits as a garnish (optional; nutritional information not included)—approximately 10 cups at 3pp per serving.

PersonalPoints

3sp or 3pp per 1 cup serving

Southwest chicken tacos

Prep Time 10 Minutes

Cook Time 4 Hrs

Total Time 4 Hrs 10 Minutes

Servings 12

Ingredients
- 1 pound boneless skinless chicken breast (about 4 breasts)
- 1 jar of salsa *15.5oz
- 1 cup frozen corn
- 1 cup diced onion
- 1 cup diced peppers
- Juice of 1 lime
- 1.5 Tbsp chili powder
- ½ tsp paprika
- Dash of salt & Pepper

Instructions

Plug the crock pot in and set it to high or low depending on how long you're cooking it for

I lightly sprayed the lowest of my crockpot, then lay down the chicken breast.

Add in the corn, peppers, and onions.

I mixed my chili powder and paprika in with the jar of salsa before pouring salsa over the fowl.

Add the lime juice, salt & Pepper, then stir the mixture around.

Cook on high for 4 hours or low for 8 hours.

Shred chicken properly in the crockpot using some forks and then served immediately.

Use your favorite low-factor taco shells and toppings, or serve on the pinnacle of a salad.

The combination on my own is 0 clever factors, the only points you will want. The number of calories you consume depends on the type of tortilla or shells and toppings you choose.

PersonalPoints

0-1PP, zero freestyle points, 1SP/1PP per serving *Blue & purple 0SP- Green 1SP

Golden chickpea and cauliflower soup

Prep Time 10 Minutes

Cook Time 4 Hrs

Total Time 4 Hrs 10 Minutes

Servings 12

Ingredients

- 1 head of cauliflower (cut into small florets)
- 3 cups dried chickpeas
- 8 cups vegetable broth
- 2 garlic cloves (diced)
- 1 Tbsp turmeric
- 1.5 tsp coriander
- Dash of salt & Pepper

Instructions

To prepare the soup, heat your crock pot and add the chickpeas, cauliflower florets, and garlic. Pour in some broth and add your preferred spices. If you have time, To prepare the dish, you can choose to cook it for 8 hours on low heat or for 4 hours on high heat. However, if you're short on time, you can cook it on high heat for 3.5 hours, followed by low heat for an hour. Make sure both the cauliflower and chickpeas are soft. After cooking, use a blender or immersion blender to blend the soup. This recipe yields 12 servings of 1 cup each. You can store it in the fridge, and it freezes well.

PersonalPoints

0SP blue & purple, 6SP/4PP per 1 cup serving

Slow cooker chicken & dumplings

Prep Time 15 Minutes

Cook Time 4 Hrs 30 Minutes

Total Time 4 Hrs 45 Minutes

Servings 10

Ingredients

- 2 lbs raw boneless skinless chicken breast (approx 32oz cut into cubes)
- 2.5 cups peeled and diced carrots
- 2 cups diced celery
- 1.5 cups diced onion
- 2 cans low fat Campbell's cream of chicken soup (284ml cans *or anything similar, brands vary in Canada/U.S)
- 2 cups chicken broth
- 1 tsp dried oregano
- 1 tsp dried thyme
- 1 bay leaf
- 2 garlic cloves (diced)
- ½ tsp each salt & Pepper
- 2 Tbsp cornstarch
- 1 package Pillsbury country biscuits *If in the U.S, you can use the small 7.5oz packages with 10 small biscuits

Instructions

Heat crock pot (excessive or low, depending on what you select for cooking time)

Cut chook into 1-2 inch dice size portions, area with inside the crock pot. Upload all diced veggies and seasonings.

Add the two cans of soup and the broth, and stir well.

If you use the 7.5oz package deal of 10 biscuits (discovered within the U.S.), use all 10, and cut every biscuit into 6. If you are in Canada and use the Pillsbury U. s. a . biscuits, use the handiest 7 of the biscuits, and reduce every biscuit into 6 pieces.

After 2.5 hours (on excessive) or 6. five hours (on low), stir within side the corn starch to thicken it up. If you cook on down, you want to show too excessive for the biscuits.

Place biscuit portions inside the crock pot, resting on the pinnacle of the stew-like mixture; make certain warmness is about too excessive when you upload the biscuits near the lid, and prepare dinner for 1-1.5 hours (VERY IMPORTANT now no longer to open the top even as The biscuits are currently cooking in the slow cooker. The cooking time may vary depending on the specific slow cooker being used. You've got the biscuits that will take 1-2 hours everywhere. Brief cooking cookers will take much less, and older fashions can also additionally take longer; in case you can't see the biscuits without casting off the lid, then take a look at them at approximately the 75-minute mark, however, be brief and if they do not appear executed quickly placed the top again on.

Makes 10 servings, approx 1 heaping cup servings. This will freeze well.

PersonalPoints 4

4P, 3SP blue/purple, 5SP green

Homemade vegetable tomato sauce

Prep Time 15 Minutes

Cook Time 6 Hrs

total time 6 Hrs 15 Minutes

Servings 12

Ingredients

- 2- 28 oz cans of crushed tomatoes
- 28 oz can diced tomatoes
- 5.5 can tomato paste
- 1 cup diced onion
- 1 small zucchini (diced)
- ½ cup diced carrots
- ½ cup diced peppers
- 2 garlic cloves (diced)
- 1 Tbsp oregano
- 1 Tbsp basil
- 1 Tbsp thyme
- 2 bay leaves
- 1 tsp paprika
- Salt & Pepper (1 tsp of each or to taste)
- ¼ cup Franks hot sauce *optional (if you want a little spice to it, I added it, and it was just enough zest but not too spicy)

Instructions

Turn the crock pot to low and place all of your ingredients in.

Cook on low for 6 hours.

I used a hand food chopper to cube all my vegetables so they have been refined and petite.

Makes 12- 1 cup servings, the only element with factors is the tomato paste; mine was 3SP for the minor can, so every 1 cup serving of this sauce is 0 points.

Store in mason jars

Cover the jars with at least 1 inch of water. Bring to a rolling boil and manner for 15 mins (20 mins for altitudes 1000 to 6000 ft, 25 mins above 6000 ft). Then flip off the heat and allow the jars to take a seat down in the warm water for five mins (those are the instructions I used while storing in mason jars, and I observed it on Google, this is as soon as you've got stuffed them with the sauce and sealed)

PersonalPoints 0

Slow cooker brisket with homemade BBQ sauce

Prep Time 5 Minutes

Cook Time 8 Hrs

Total Time 8 Hrs 5 Minutes

Servings 12

Ingredients

- 3-4 lb lean brisket (mine was approx 3.5lbs)
- RUB
- 1 Tbsp brown sugar
- ½ tsp mustard powder
- ½ tsp cumin
- 1 tsp garlic powder
- 1 tsp dried oregano
- 1 tsp paprika
- 1 tsp cajun seasoning
- Salt & Pepper (to liking)

BBQ SAUCE

- ¼ cup brown sugar
- 1/3 cup apple cider vinegar
- 2 Tbsp mustard
- 2/3 cup ketchup
- 2 Tbsp Worcestershire sauce
- 2 Tbsp franks hot sauce (optional)
- 2 tsp chili powder
- 1 tsp garlic powder
- 1/4 tsp cayenne pepper

Instructions

Plug in the crock pot and flip to low. (*you could prepare dinner on excessive and test Brisket at about 4-5 hours. However, I decide to gradual cooking it)

Mix all of your rub substances collectively and rub evenly over your Brisket (* if time lets in, you could wrap it in saran and allow sit in the fridge for some hours or even overnight)

In a Cup, mix your BBQ sauce substances collectively.

Place brisket in the crock pot and pour BBQ sauce over your meat.

Let's prepare dinner on low for at least eight hours.

Briskets have to shred without problems with a fork. Serve together with your preferred facet dish. I made garlic parmesan potatoes (recipe for the ones coming soon)

I changed into being capable of getting 12- 3oz servings, and I find declaring meat cooked in sauce in the gradual cooker difficult; manifestly, you only consume some of the sauce this is in the pot. I am leaving the dietary info for the sauce only; Brisket is 4SP in keeping with a 3oz serving. I might count for 1-2 factors for the sauce, relying on how "saucy" you're making your serving.

PersonalPoints 3oz of Brisket is 4SP

Creamy tomato tortellini soup

Prep Time 10 Minutes

Cook Time 1 Hrs 30 Minutes

Total Time 1 Hrs 40 Minutes

Servings 10

Ingredients
- 2 cans of condensed light tomato soup (picture below)
- 2 Tbsp tomato paste
- 3.5 cups vegetable broth
- 1.5 cups milk (I used 1%)
- 3/4 cup soft cream (like a half & half (I used 5%))
- 1 cup diced red onion
- 2 garlic cloves (diced)
- Salt & Pepper to taste
- 1 tsp dried oregano
- 1 tsp Italian seasoning
- 3.5 cups cheese tortellini (picture below)
- 2 Tbsp finely grated parmesan cheese

Instructions
Turn crock pot to high (you may use a large pot on the stove properly in case you wish, I might turn it to med-high)

Add in your tomato soup and paste and stir.

Mix in your diced garlic and onion. Stir in vegetable broth, milk, and cream, after which your seasonings and dash of salt & Pepper.

Cook on high for a half-hour, stir for your raw tortellini, and prepare dinner on high for 1 hour. Turn to low and stir in your parmesan cheese.

Serve heat while ready. I also made a few clean low-factor croutons for topping, preheated oven to 375F, split low-factor bread (Sara Lee multigrain), and assorted bread with a few salt, Pepper, and garlic salt. Place on a baking sheet blanketed with parchment paper and sprayed with a few butter-flavored cooking sprays, toss round, then toast in the Oven for approx 10 minutes. Including some soup may not affect factors placed in case you upload equal to a chunk of bread, then upload 1 factor.

PersonalPoints 5PP, 5SP green, blue & purple

Chicken parmesan lasagna rolls

Prep Time 15 Minutes

Cook Time 25 Minutes

Total Time 40 Minutes

Servings 8

Ingredients

- 8 cooked lasagna noodles
- 12 oz cooked shredded chicken (about 3 cups)
- 1 ¾ cups light tomato pasta sauce
- 2/3 cup shredded creamy mozzarella
- 4 Tbsp grated parmesan cheese
- 2 Tbsp bread crumbs
- Dried parsley

Instructions

Boil and drain your lasagna noodles

Preheat Oven to 350F and spray a casserole dish (I used a 9x13)

Mix your shredded chicken (I cook mine in the crock pot in a bit of broth on excessive for approximately three hours, it will shred nicely) with 3/4 cups of pasta sauce.

Lay out your noodles and place approximately four Tbsp of hen aggregate on every noodle; use a knife to unfold the entirety; then sprinkle 1 tsp of parmesan cheese on top of the total and roll the noodle up.

Place on your casserole dish. Once all 8 rolls are made, pour 1 cup of pasta sauce over the rolls.

Sprinkle your shredded mozzarella, remaining parmesan, and bread crumbs on the pinnacle of the sauce, ideal with dried parsley.

Bake in the Oven for approx 25 minutes, making 8 rolls.

PersonalPoints 2-5PP, 4SP blue, 5SP green, 2SP purple if using whole wheat pasta

Slow Cooker Teriyaki Chicken

Prep Time 5 Minutes

Cook Time 4 Hrs

Total Time 4 Hrs 5 Minutes

Serving 6

EQUIPMENT
- Slow Cooker

Ingredients
- 2½ lbs boneless skinless chicken breast cut into 2-inch pieces
- ½ cup honey
- 3 cloves garlic
- ½ cup soy sauce

Instructions

Combine chicken, honey, garlic, and soy sauce in a slow cooker. Set the slow cooker to the low setting, then cover it.

for two hours before stirring. 2 more hours (for a total of 4 hours) of cooking

Discard the garlic and serve.

PersonalPoints 7

6 Blue Plan and 9 Green Plan

Beef Stew

Serves 8

Ingredients
- 2 lbs beef chuck tender roast, raw trimmed of fat, and cut into 1" cubes
- 4 stalks of celery chopped into chunky pieces
- 4 large carrots chopped into chunky pieces
- 1 medium sweet onion chopped into chunky pieces
- 2 cups corn canned, fresh, or frozen
- 3 cloves garlic roughly chopped
- 6 tbs flour divided
- 1 cup low-sodium beef broth
- 3 tbsp Worcestershire sauce
- 3 sprigs of fresh thyme
- 1 tbsp brown sugar
- 8 oz tomato sauce canned
- 2 bay leaves

Instructions

Add raw red meat chunks to the slow cooker. Salt and pepper the beef chunks well. To prepare the meat, sprinkle 3 tablespoons of flour over it. Stir until the beef is covered. (reserve the other 3 tablespoons for later)

Add chopped celery, onions, carrots, garlic, thyme, bay leaves, tomato sauce, Worcestershire sauce, and brown sugar. Stir collectively well. (Do now no longer upload corn)

Cook on low for 8-9 hours. Slow and occasional is best for tender red meat; however, you may prepare dinner on high for 5-6 hours.

When the stew is done cooking, add the corn and stir together.

In a small cup, upload 3 tablespoons of flour and three tablespoons of water. Whisk collectively till there aren't any clumps. Add into the stew and stir together until the hash feels thicker. Cook on low for about 30 minutes to ensure the raw flour flavor is cooked off. Salt & Pepper to taste!! Remove thyme sprigs and bay leaves.

For maximum deliciousness, serve the stew over mashed potatoes or my favorite Home style Cauli Tater Mash! Enjoy!

PersonalPoints 5

Burrito Cup

Prep Time 10 Minutes

Cook Time 35 Minutes

Total Time 45 Minutes

Serving 6

Ingredients
- 1 medium onion finely chopped
- 1 medium bell pepper finely chopped
- 1 tsp onion powder/granules
- 1 tsp garlic powder/granules
- 1 tsp dried oregano
- 2 tsp ground cumin
- 1.5 tsp paprika
- 0.5 tsp cayenne pepper
- 0.5 tsp salt
- 0.25 tsp ground black pepper
- 1 tbsp vegetable oil
- 16 oz ground beef - 5% fat (450g)
- 1 can black beans 1 x 15oz / 425g can (drained)
- 1 can sweetcorn 1 x 8.5oz / 248g can (drained)
- 1 can diced tomatoes 1 x 15oz / 425g can
- 1 cup rice (*brown if following Purple plan) (200g)
- 1 stock cube/bouillon cube, either beef or vegetable

- 2 cups water (240ml)

Instructions

Chop the onion and Pepper into small portions and set aside.

Mix the onion powder, garlic powder, oregano, cumin, paprika, cayenne Pepper, salt, and Pepper right into a small cup and set aside.

Heat the oil in a big skillet over medium heat.

Add the chopped onions and peppers and saute for 6 - 8 minutes, stirring often, until they soften.

Add the ground pork and use a timber spoon or fork to break it up.

Cook for 6 - 8 mins until the pork has cooked and lost its pinkness.

Add the spice mix, stir, and cook for 1 minute before including the beans, corn, and canned tomatoes.

Stir well so that it's far all combined.

Dissolve the inventory cube/bouillon in the 2 cups of warm water and upload to the mixture.

Finally, stir in the rice.

Give the mixture a great stir and convey it to the boil.

Reduce the warmth, then depart to simmer for 15 - 20 mins (stirring regularly to save you if it is sticking to the pan) till most of the liquid has been absorbed by the rice.

Remove from the heat and serve hot.

PersonalPoints

Freestyle Plan - 6 SmartPoint Blue Plan - 6 Green Plan - 8 Purple Plan - 3

Taco Turkey Lettuce Wraps

Prep Time 5 Minutes

Cook Time 10 Minutes

Total Time 15 Minutes

Ingredients
- 2 teaspoons olive oil
- ¾ cups chopped yellow onion
- 1 pound ground turkey we use 93% lean
- 1 cup salsa (equivalent to 1 14-ounce jar)
- 1 tablespoons taco seasoning
- 2-3 heads of butter lettuce. Other lettuce suggestions in the notes

Instructions

In a big skillet, heat the oil over medium-high heat.

Add the onions when the oil's surface ripples—Sauté for 3 to 4 minutes or until transparent.

When there is no longer any pink tint, add the ground turkey and simmer, stirring often. Break the turkey into little pieces as it cooks.

Stir in the salsa and taco seasoning after adding them. To enable the flavors to meld, cook for 1-2 minutes. Get rid of the heat.

Onto each large lettuce leaf, spoon ¼ cup of the taco meat. Choose your toppings, then indulge!

PersonalPoints 2

Green: 1 Blue: 1 Purple: 1

Thai Chicken ww Recipe

Prep Time 20 Minutes

Cook Time 20 Minutes

Total Time 40 Minutes

Ingredients

- 4-5 boneless skinless thin sliced chicken breasts
- Salt and black Pepper, to taste
- ½ cup Thai chili sauce
- 2 fresh limes juiced
- ¼ cup soy sauce
- 3 tbsp peanut butter
- 1 tbsp grated ginger
- 1 tbsp garlic, minced
- 2 bell peppers, red and orange, stemmed and chopped
- 1 cup broccoli, separated into florets
- 2 cups snow peas
- 1 cup carrots, sliced round
- ½ onion, diced
- 2 tbsp olive oil.
- Lime wheels, to top
- ¼ cup peanuts, chopped.
- Fresh cilantro

Instructions

Preheat the Oven to 400°F.

2. Place the hen in a big, seal-cabin a position plastic bag.

3. In a Cup, upload the candy Thai chili sauce, lime juice, soy sauce, peanut butter, ginger, and garlic.

4. Stir to combine.

5. Pour ¾ of the sauce into the seal cap in a position bag with the hen.

6. Shake the bag and cowl the hen to marinate for two hours.

7. Remove the hen from the bag and vicinity the hen on a parchment-protected baking sheet.

8. In a big Cup, upload the peppers, broccoli, snow peas, carrots, and onion.

9. Add the olive oil and the relaxation of the Thai peanut sauce.

10. Season the whole lot with salt and Pepper.

11. Place the greens across the hen and pinnacle with lime wheels.

12. Bake for 20 minutes or till hen is cooked.

13. Make sure the greens are tender.

14. Sprinkle the dish with the overwhelmed peanuts

15. Top with cilantro.

Serve as is for 5 factors, or serve with rice and rely on the more significant factors!

PersonalPoints

4 Blue Plan and 5 Green Plan

4 WW Freestyle Points and 5 Smart Points

Chicken Pineapple Stir-Fry

Prep Time 7 Minutes

Cook Time 15 Minutes

Total Time 22 Minutes

Serving 6

EQUIPMENT
- Skillet
- Large Cup
- Small Cup

Ingredients
- ¼ cup soy sauce
- 2 tbsp sugar
- 1 tbsp cider vinegar
- 1 tbsp ketchup
- ½ tsp ginger
- 1 tbsp garlic – minced
- 1 tsp cornstarch
- 8 oz pineapple chunks drained; reserve ¼ cup juice
- 1 lb boneless skinless chicken breast in 2-inch strips

- 2 tbsp vegetable oil
- 16 oz frozen stir fry vegetables
- hot cooked rice as needed

Instructions

Combine ¼ Cup of the saved pineapple juice with the soy sauce, sugar, vinegar, ketchup, ginger, minced garlic, and cornstarch in a small Cup.

Pan with oil in it. Heat

Chicken is stir-fried in heated oil for approximately 5 minutes in a big skillet. Add the frozen vegetables and stir-fry for another 4 minutes.

The sauce and pineapple. Add stirring, then fully warm.

She was serving with rice.

PersonalPoints

4 Blue Plan and 5 Green Plan

4 WW Freestyle Points 5 Smart Points

Teriyaki Chicken Sheet Pan

Prep Time 10 Mins

Cook Time 40 Mins

Total Time 50 mins

Servings 4

Ingredients

- 1 cup soy sauce
- 3 T honey
- 3 T rice vinegar
- 3 tsp sesame oil divided
- 3 tsp minced garlic or 2 tsp dry
- 1 t grated ginger or ½ tsp dry
- 1 T cornstarch
- ¼ cup water
- 2 lbs chicken breasts – cut in half lengthways to speed cooking
- 3 C broccoli florets
- 1 C carrots sliced on diagonal
- ¼ cup edamame shelled
- Sesame seeds for garnish optional

Instructions

Heat cooking oil in a big pan over medium heat. Stir fry chicken, stirring occasionally, till lightly browned and crisp.

Combine the soy sauce, sugar, Sake/vinegar, Mirin, and sesame oil in a small jug or cup. Set aside.

Add the garlic to the center of the pan and saute till lightly fragrant (approximately 30 seconds). Pour in the sauce and permit to cook, while stirring, till the sauce thickens right into a lovely vivid glaze (approximately 2-3 minutes)

Add in the steamed broccoli. Garnish with green onion (or shallot) slices and serve over steamed rice.

PersonalPoints 0

Easy Chicken Corn Chowder

Prep Time 25 Mins

Cook Time 15 Mins

Total Time 40 Mins

Servings 6

Ingredients
- 1 tablespoon butter
- ½ Cup finely chopped onion
- ½ Cup finely chopped celery
- 1 medium jalapeno pepper, seeded and minced
- 2 tablespoons all-purpose flour
- 3 cups 2% milk
- 2 cups chopped roasted, skinless, boneless chicken breasts
- One 14.75-ounce can cream style corn
- 1½ cups frozen corn kernels (or 3 ears of fresh corn)
- 1½ teaspoons chopped fresh thyme
- ½ teaspoon salt
- ⅛ teaspoon ground red pepper

Instructions
In a sizable pot set over medium heat, melt the butter. Add the onion, celery, and jalapeno. Stir regularly for 3 minutes or until cooked.

Add the flour and whisk continuously for 1 minute. Add the milk and the remaining ingredients and stir.

Bring to a boil, then simmer for five minutes or until thick.

PersonalPoints 0

Chickpea & Feta Salad

Prep Time 20 Mins

Cook Time 0 Mins

Total Time 20 Mins

Servings 6

Ingredients

- 2 cups canned chickpeas, rinsed and drained
- 1-2 garlic cloves, or to taste, finely minced
- 3 tablespoons thinly sliced scallions
- ½ large sweet red bell pepper, diced
- ½ Cup diced English cucumber
- 2 tablespoons fresh, finely minced parsley
- 9 large black or green olives, pitted and roughly chopped
- ½ cup crumbled feta cheese
- 3 tablespoons fresh lemon juice
- 1 tablespoon olive oil
- Salt and freshly ground black Pepper to taste
- 1 teaspoon lemon zest, for garnish (optional)

Instructions

Melt the butter in a large pot over medium heat. Add the celery, onion, and jalapeno and simmer for 3 minutes, stirring frequently.

Whisk continuously for 1 minute after adding the flour. Stir in the other ingredients, including the milk.

To thicken, simmer for five minutes after bringing to a boil.

PersonalPoints

5 SmartPoints (Green plan) 2 SmartPoints (Blue plan)

2 SmartPoints (Purple plan) 4 PointsPlus (Old plan)

Egg Roll in a Cup

Prep Time 10 Mins

Total Time 10 Mins

Yield 6

Ingredients
- 1 tsp minced ginger
- 4 1/2 cups (s) packaged coleslaw mix (shredded cabbage and carrots)
- 1/2 cup(s) shredded carrots
- 3 medium scallions
- 3 Tbsp low sodium soy sauce
- 1 1/2 teaspoon sesame oil
- 1 pound(s) ground chicken breast (98% FF)

Instructions
Add the ginger after browning your preferred meat in a medium nonstick skillet until thoroughly cooked.

Add sesame oil and soy sauce.

Add the entire bag of slaw and mix to coat with the sauce.

Add a half cup of the shredded carrots, then toss them in the sauce.

Add the chopped scallions, combine them, and cook the cole slaw over high heat until it is reduced by half.

PersonalPoints 0

Healthy Chicken Salad with Apples & Cranberries

Prep Time 10 Mins

Cook Time 0 Mins

Total Time 10 Mins

Servings 4

Ingredients
- 2 ½ cups chopped cooked chicken
- 3 stalks of celery, chopped
- 1 cup chopped apple, about 1 large; I used a Pink Lady and kept the peel because it was organic
- ¼ cup dried cranberries
- ½ cup nonfat plain Greek yogurt
- 2 tablespoons Hellman's light mayonnaise
- 2 teaspoons lemon juice
- 2 tablespoons chopped parsley (optional)

- Salt and Pepper to taste

Instructions

Stir the chicken, celery, apple, and cranberries in a Cup before setting it aside.

Combine the yogurt, mayonnaise, and lemon juice in a small Cup.

Stir well before adding it to the chicken mixture.

If preferred, stir in the parsley. Use salt and Pepper to taste to season.

PersonalPoints

5 SmartPoints (Green plan) 3 SmartPoints (Blue plan)

3 SmartPoints (Purple plan) 5 PointsPlus (Old plan)

Sheet Pan Chicken Fajitas

Prep Time 10 Mins

Cook Time 15 Mins

Total Time 25 Mins

Ingredients

- 1lb chicken, cut into thin strips
- ½ each- green, red, orange, and yellow bell pepper- thinly sliced
- ½ red onion- thinly sliced
- 1 tablespoon olive oil
- 2 jalapeno- deseeded and diced
- 1 lime
- 8-10 6" Flour Tortillas
- Seasoning
- 1 tsp chili powder
- ¼ tsp cayenne
- 1 tsp paprika
- 1 tsp onion powder
- 1 tsp garlic powder
- 1 ½ tsp cumin
- ½ tsp coriander
- 1 tsp sea salt & Pepper

Instructions

The Oven to 425 degrees.

Add all the fajita ingredients and 1 tablespoon olive oil to a Cup. Mix thoroughly.

Chicken and vegetables are stirred in. Mix thoroughly to coat equally.

Avoid crowding the pan with too many chicken pieces, or they won't get crispy.

Vegetables should be arranged around the pan's edges.

For 15 minutes, bake. For the final five minutes of cooking the chicken, wrap the tortillas in foil and heat in the Oven.

PersonalPoints 0

Cajun Chicken and Rice

Total Time 40 Mins

Servings 4

EQUIPMENT
- Nonstick skillet

Ingredients
- 1 tsp olive oil
- 1 clove garlic minced
- ½ green bell pepper chopped
- 1 onion chopped
- ½ tsp ground cumin
- 1 tsp chili powder
- 2 tsp cajun seasoning
- ⅓ Cup long-grain brown rice
- ½ cup water
- 14½ oz canned stewed tomatoes
- 4 pimento-stuffed olives halved
- 1 cup cooked chicken cubed

Instructions
Oil should be heated at medium-high heat in a medium nonstick skillet.

Cook garlic, onion, and green pepper over medium heat for about 8 minutes, stirring frequently, or until the vegetables are soft.

Add Cajun seasoning, chili powder, and cumin to the skillet—about 1 minute of stirring and cooking.

Place the rice in the skillet and stir for about a minute or until the grains are coated.

Bring to a boil the tomatoes and water in the skillet.

For 15 minutes, simmer with the lid on.

Cook covered for about 5 minutes, or until the chicken is hot and the rice is done, by adding the chicken and the olives to a skillet.

PersonalPoints

2 Blue Plan and 6 Green Plan

2 WW Freestyle Points and 6 WW Smart Points

Best Chicken Salad

Prep Time 15 Mins

Total Time 15 Mins

Servings 6

Ingredients

- 3 cups chicken - cooked & chopped (400g)
- 3 - 4 stalks celery
- 3 green onions/spring onions
- 1 ½ cups grapes (225g)
- 1 - 1 ½ tsp dijon mustard
- ⅓ cup reduced-fat mayonnaise (75g)
- ½ Cup fat-free natural yogurt (120g)
- Salt & pepper

Instructions

Add the chicken to a medium Cup once it has been torn up or sliced into bite-sized pieces.

Cut the celery into small pieces after trimming the ends, then add it to the chicken.

Green onions should be diced and added to the Cup.

Depending on the size of the grapes you use, chop them in half and combine them with the other ingredients.

Combine the mustard, mayonnaise, and plain yogurt in a small Cup.

Mix the remaining ingredients gently after spooning the mayonnaise dressing over them.

To taste, add salt and Pepper.

She was serving and keeping track!

PersonalPoints

Blue plan – 1 Freestyle plan – 1 Green plan – 3 Purple plan – 1

Whole Wheat Pumpkin Muffins

Prep Time 20 Minutes

Cook Time 12 Minutes

Total Time 35 Minutes

Ingredients

- 1 and 3/4 Cup of (220g) whole wheat flour* (spoon & leveled)
- 1 tsp baking powder
- 1 tsp baking soda
- ½ tsp salt
- 1 tsp ground cinnamon
- 1 tsp store-bought or homemade pumpkin pie spice*
- 2 large eggs at room temperature
- ½ Cup of (95g) lightly packed brown sugar
- 1 Cup of (228g) pumpkin puree (not pumpkin pie filling)
- 1/3 Cup of (72g) unsalted butter, melted and slightly cooled*
- 1 tsp pure vanilla extract
- 1/3 Cup of (80ml) milk (I use almond milk; any milk is OK)
- ½ Cup of (90g) minced chocolate chips*

Instructions

The oven should be heated to 350°F (177°C). Apply nonstick cooking spray to two small muffin pans to grease or spray. You will only need half of the second pan because this recipe yields around 36 muffins. Use cooking spray to grease or spray micro liners. Discard the pans.

The flour, baking powder, baking soda, salt, cinnamon, and pumpkin pie spice should all be combined in a big basin. Place aside. Eggs, brown sugar, pumpkin puree, melted butter, vanilla, and milk should all be mixed in a medium basin. The wet components should be added to the dry ingredients and combined several times before the chocolate chips are added. Gently fold everything together until incorporated.

Fill muffin tins between 3/4 and full. For each muffin, aim for around 1 heaping Tsp of batter. 12 to 14 minutes of baking time, or until a toothpick inserted in the center of the cake comes out clean. Make careful to move the pans during the baking process if your oven has hot areas. The muffins I made took 12 minutes. From the oven, remove the pans. Before eating, let the muffins somewhat cool.

Creamy Chicken Enchiladas

Prep Time 15 Minutes

Cook Time 10 Minutes

Total Time 25 Minutes

Ingredients

- 1 Tsp olive oil
- ½ Cup of chopped onion (1 medium)
- 2 tsp finely chopped garlic
- 2 Cup of Progresso™ reduced-sodium chicken broth (from 32-oz carton)
- 3 Tsp Gold Medal™ all-purpose flour
- 1/2 tsp ground coriander or minced
- 1/8 tsp pepper
- 1/2 Cup of reduced-fat sour cream
- 2 Cup of shredded cooked chicken breast
- 1 Cup of Green Giant frozen corn, thawed
- 1 Cup of shredded reduced-fat Mexican cheese blend (4 oz)
- 1 can (4.5 oz) chopped green chiles
- 1/4 Cup of chopped fresh cilantro
- 8 corn or flour tortillas (6 or 7 inches)
- 1 medium tomato, chopped (3/4 Cup of)
- 4 medium green onions, sliced (1/4 Cup of)
- Salsa, if desired

Instructions

350°F oven temperature. Cooking sprays a 13 by 9-inch (3-quart) glass baking dish.

Heat oil in a 10-inch nonstick skillet over medium heat. When the onion is soft, add the onion and garlic and simmer for 3 to 4 minutes, stirring regularly. Use a wire whisk to thoroughly combine the broth, flour, coriander, and Pepper in a medium bowl. Add slowly while continuously swirling the heated mixture in the skillet. Cook and whisk for 5 to 6 minutes, or until mixture begins to boil and slightly thickens. Get rid of the heat. Add the sour cream and mix thoroughly.

Combine the chicken, Corn, chiles, cilantro, 1/2 cup of cheese, and the remaining sauce in a separate medium bowl. On a microwaveable dish, place two tortillas at once and cover them with a paper towel. 10 to 15 seconds on high in the microwave or until softened. The middle of each cooked tortilla should contain about 1/3 cup of the chicken mixture. Wrap tortillas in a roll, then place seam-side down in a baking dish. Finish enchiladas with any extra sauce. Wrap with foil.

Until the sauce is bubbling, bake for 30 to 35 minutes. Take it out of the oven. Remove the lid and top with the final 1/2 Cup of cheese. Before serving, let it stand for a while. Add tomato and green onions to the top just before acting. Accompanied by salsa.

Crispy Parmesan Chicken Strips

Prep Time15 Minutes

Cook Time10 Minutes

Total Time25 Minutes

Ingredients

- 1 1/2 Cup of (375 mL) seasoned croutons, crushed
- 1 1/2 oz (45 g) grated fresh Parmesan cheese (about 1/2 Cup of/125 mL packed)
- 1 tsp (5 mL) dried parsley
- 1/4 tsp (1 mL) garlic salt
- 2 egg whites
- 1 tbsp (15 mL) water
- 1 lb (500 g) boneless, skinless chicken breasts, cut into 1-in. (2.5-cm) strips

Instructions

The oven should be heated to 450°F (230°C).

Combine the croutons, cheese, parsley, and garlic salt in a medium bowl.

In a separate bowl, whisk together egg whites and water.

Each chicken strip should be equally coated after being dipped in the egg and crouton mixture.

Place the strips on a Medium Round Stone with Handles in a single layer.

Bake the chicken for 14 to 16 minutes until the middle is no longer pink.

Easy White Chicken Chili

Prep Time 5 Minutes

Cook Time 4 Hours

Total Time 4 Hrs 5 Minutes

Ingredients

- 2 lbs chicken breast
- 2 tsp minced
- 1 tsp garlic powder
- 1 tsp onion powder
- Salt and pepper
- 14 oz. canned pinto beans drained and rinsed
- 14 oz. canned white beans drained and rinsed
- 14 oz. canned corn, drained and rinsed
- 16 oz green salsa
- 4 Cup of fat-free chicken broth

Instructions

Stir everything into the slow cooker after adding it all. Cook the chicken thoroughly for 4 hours on low heat. Take the chicken out and cut or shred it. Bring the soup back to the table.

Everything should be placed in the Instant Pot. After the broth has finished cooking, you can add additional if you've reached the maximum fill line. For eight minutes, on manual. Allow the Instant Pot to release typically. Take the chicken out and cut or shred it. Re-add to the chili, then dish up. Then top it with all of your preferred chili-related garnishes.

Stovetop:

Place all the ingredients in a large soup pot or Dutch oven.

After bringing to a simmer, cook for 25–30 minutes.

Remove and shred or chop the chicken once it has finished cooking.

Reintroduce to the chili, then serve.

Friendly Chicken Cordon Bleu

Prep Time 10 Minutes

Cook Time 6 Hrs

Total Time 6 Hrs 10 Minutes

Ingredients

- 4 boneless, skinless chicken breasts (8 halves)
- 8 slices Hillshire Farm Deli Select Ham, thick slices
- 1 ½ Cup of shredded fat-free mozzarella cheese
- 2/3 Cup of skim milk
- 1 Cup of finely crushed Corn Flakes
- ½ tsp Italian Seasoning
- ½ tsp ground black pepper
- 1 tsp of this spice
- ½ tsp salt
- 1 can (10.75 ounces) Campbell's Healthy Request Cream of Chicken Soup – unprepared
- ½ Cup of fat-free sour cream
- Juice of half a lemon

Instructions

Turn the oven on to 350 degrees.

Pound chicken breast halves to a thickness of about ¼ inch.

Chicken breasts should be seasoned with salt and Pepper.

Each breast should have a piece of ham on top and roughly 3 Tsp of cheese running down the center.

Each breast is rolled up, with the ends tucked in and fastened with toothpicks.

Fill a basin with milk so that it will be simple to dip the breasts in it.

The finely crushed cornflakes, smoked paprika, and Italian spice should all be together on a platter. You may also combine it in a bowl before pouring it onto a dish.

Take each breast and roll it in the milk, followed by the cornflakes.

Apply cooking spray to a baking pan.

Bake chicken breasts in a baking dish for 25 to 30 minutes at 350 degrees or until a meat thermometer registers 165 degrees.

Combine the soup, sour cream, and lemon juice in a pan and heat until the chicken is almost done.

Once the chicken has finished roasting, please remove it from the oven and remove the toothpicks.

Include two tsp of cream sauce with each breast.

Easy Taco Salad

Prep Time 10 Minutes

Cook Time 6 hr

Total Time 6 hr 10 Minutes

Ingredients

- 12 ounces ground round
- 2 Cup of chopped yellow, red, or green bell pepper
- 2 Cup of bottled salsa
- 1/4 Cup of chopped fresh cilantro
- 4 Cup of coarsely chopped romaine lettuce
- 2 Cup of chopped plum tomato
- 1 Cup of (4 ounces) shredded reduced-fat sharp cheddar cheese
- 1 Cup of crumbled baked tortilla chips (about 12 chips)
- 1/4 Cup of chopped green onions

Instructions

Over medium-high heat, cook the meat and bell pepper in a large nonstick pan until the steak is browned. Stir to crumble. Salsa added; bring to a boil. Add the cilantro and keep it heated.

Place one Cup of lettuce and one Cup of the meat mixture on each of the four dishes. For garnish, add 1/2 Cup of tomato, 1/4 Cup of cheese, 1/4 Cup of chips, and 1 Tsp onion to each word.

Contains 4 equal servings.

Chili in the Crock Pot

Prep Time 15 Minutes

Cook Time 4 hours

Total Time 4 hours 15 minutes

Ingredients

- 1 pound 99% fat-free ground chicken
- 1 can of Kidney beans drained (15 oz)
- 1 can diced tomatoes with green chiles 14.5 oz
- 1 can dice tomatoes 14.5 oz
- 1 small onion chopped
- 1 Tsp chili powder
- 1 tsp minced
- ¼ tsp cayenne pepper
- ¼ tsp garlic powder
- 1 tsp salt

Instructions

In a pan, cook ground chicken while crumbling it into little pieces.

In a crock pot, combine chicken, kidney beans, two cans of diced tomatoes, chopped onion, and seasonings.

Combine the ingredients by stirring.

Cook for 4 hours on high in a crock pot.

Baked Cream Cheese Spaghetti Casserole

Prep Time 10 Minutes

Cook Time 20 Minutes

Total Time 30 Minutes

Ingredients
- 12 oz spaghetti
- 1 (28 ounce) jar of prepared spaghetti sauce
- 1 lb lean ground beef lean ground turkey
- 1 tsp Italian seasoning
- 1 clove garlic, minced
- 8 ounces cream cheese fat-free cream cheese
- ½ Cup of parmesan cheese, grated

Instructions
Oven to 350 degrees Fahrenheit.

Spaghetti sauce is added after the ground beef has been cooked thoroughly and the fat drained. Place aside.

Follow the packet's instructions while cooking spaghetti. Put cooked spaghetti in a basin after draining. Add cream cheese, minutes garlic, and Italian seasoning. Stir the spaghetti until it is well coated with cream cheese and melted.

Grease a 9" x 13" pan sparingly. The dish's base should be covered with a thin layer of beef sauce. The leftover meat sauce should then be topped with the noodles. On top, grate some parmesan cheese.

Bake the bubbling mixture for 30 minutes.

Chicken Salad Recipe

Prep Time 10 Minutes

Cook Time 20 Minutes

Total Time 30 Minutes

Ingredients
- 2 pounds cooked boneless, skinless chicken breast
- 1 Cup of purple grapes, halved
- 2 TBS chives, scallions or green onion
- 5 ribs celery, washed and chopped
- 1 TSP of this seasoning (click here)
- ½ Cup of light mayonnaise
- ½ Cup of plain, nonfat Greek yogurt

Instructions

Chicken breasts should be cooked through. You may bake in the oven or use nonstick cooking spray for pan frying.

Use a knife to cut or shred the chicken. Place in a mixing dish of medium Size.

Grapes must be washed and sliced in half. Put into the basin. Wash and chop chives. Put into the bay.

Cut and wash the celery. Put into the basin.

To the bowl, add garlic powder.

Greek yogurt and light mayonnaise are added to the dish.

If the dish tastes extra, add a dash or two of this spice.

Before serving, thoroughly combine and refrigerate for an hour.

Hamburger Stroganoff

Prep Time 5 Minutes

Cook Time 20 Minutes

Total Time 25 Minutes

Ingredients

- 8 ounces lean ground beef
- ½ Cup of chopped onion
- 2 Cup of egg noodles prepared
- 10 ¾ ounce 98& fat-free cream of mushroom soup canned
- 4 oz canned sliced mushrooms
- ¼ Cup of low-fat sour cream
- salt and Pepper to taste

Instructions

Drain grease after browning ground meat and onion.

Add salt, Pepper, cream of mushroom soup, cooked noodles, and mushroom slices after stirring.

Roughly 5–10 minutes to simmer.

Before serving, remove from the heat and mix in the sour cream.

Tortilla Pepperoni Pizza

Prep Time 5 Minutes

Cook Time 5 Minutes

Total Time 10 Minutes

Ingredients

- 1 La Tortilla Factory Low Carb Whole Wheat Tortilla
- 2 ounces Trader Joe's Lite Mozzarella
- 3 Tsp marinara sauce
- 1/4 tsp dried oregano
- 1 pinch of crushed red Pepper
- 8 slices turkey pepperoni
- 1 spray canola oil spray

Instructions

Set the oven's temperature to 425.

Spread the marinara on the tortilla, then assemble your pizza.

Add the pepperoni after the mozzarella cheese.

Add oregano and red pepper flakes over the top.

Spray the canola oil high-speed (a half-second spray)

Bake until bubbling and golden, about 5-7 minutes.

Observe for two to three minutes before eating.

Deli Crab Salad

Prep Time 3 hrs 15 Minutes

Total Time 3 hrs 15 Minutes

Ingredients

- 6 ounces imitation crab meat
- 2 Tsp light mayo
- Chopped green onion or chives
- ½ to 1 tsp mustard
- ¼ Cup of fat-free sour cream
- onion powder to taste
- salt and Pepper to taste
- 1 Cup of cooked macaroni noodles

Instructions

1 Cup of cooked noodles is measured out. To cool the noodles:

Submerge them in cold water.

Combine the pasta and the crab meat in either shredded or chopped form.

Add chives or green onions.

Combine the remaining ingredients in a separate bowl.

Add sauce to the spaghetti mixture and thoroughly combine.

Place the flavors in the refrigerator for several hours or overnight to allow the flavors to meld.

Broccoli Cheese Soup

Prep Time 5 Minutes

Cook Time 5 Minutes

Total Time 10 Minutes

Ingredients

- 3 (14 ½ ounce) cans of chicken broth
- 2 (1 lb) bags of frozen broccoli
- 1 (10 1/2 ounce) cans rote brand tomatoes and green chilies
- 10 ounces Velveeta reduced-fat cheese product

Instructions

Combine tomatoes, chiles, frozen broccoli, and chicken broth.

Vegetables should be soft after 25 minutes of simmering.

Put the cubed Velveeta in the soup pot.

Just let the cheese melt while simmering.

This dish freezes and stores nicely in the fridge. I prepare a sizable dish at the start of the week and eat it as a snack when I'm about to stray from my diet. I can have a substantial bowl of food and some crusty bread and stay under 5 points.

Tuna and Egg Salad

Prep Time 5 Minutes

Cook Time 5 Minutes

Total Time 10 Minutes

Ingredients

- 12 oz of tuna packed in water
- 4 hard-boiled eggs
- 3 tbsp of light mayonnaise
- 2 tbs of prepared yellow mustard
- Dash of Pepper
- Salt may be added, but there should be enough salt in the canned tuna.

Instructions

Cook four eggs. Chop hard-boiled eggs and add to a dish of batter. Combine eggs with the remaining ingredients.

Use on a sandwich or a bed of lettuce.

¼ Cup of is one serving (enough for a sandwich)

Chili Recipe for ZERO

Prep Time 10 Minutes

Cook Time 25 Minutes

Total Time 35 Minutes

Ingredients

- 1 lb Ground lean chicken or ground lean turkey
- 2 15 oz cans kidney beans (drained and rinsed)
- 2 15 oz cans of black beans (drained and rinsed)
- 2 15 oz cans of pinto beans (drained and rinsed)
- 3 10 oz cans Rote Original Diced Tomatoes & Green Chilies
- 1 15 oz can tomato sauce
- ½ T minced
- ½ T oregano
- 1 T chili powder
- 2-3 cloves garlic
- 1 onion, diced
- 1 lime, quartered

Instructions

Your pressure cooker or Instant Pot should be filled with lean ground meat. To cook the beef, utilize your device's Sauté or Brown mode.

Except for the lime, add the remaining ingredients to the pressure cooker. Slice a lime in half, then squeeze the juice into a saucepan. Throw away the rind.

Choose the Meat/Stew or Beans/Chili button. Start up your device. Ensure that the pressure valve is shut. Depending on the machine you use (my cooks in 20 minutes), it will take 20 to 35 minutes to cook.

Your cooker's pressure should be released before you serve.

Taco Turkey Lettuce Wraps

Prep Time 5 Minutes

Cook Time 10 Minutes

Total Time 15 Minutes

Ingredients

- 2 tsp olive oil
- ¾ Cup of chopped yellow onion
- 1 pound ground turkey we use 93% lean
- 1 Cup of salsa (the equivalent of 1 14-ounce jar)
- 1 Tsp taco seasoning
- 2-3 heads of butter lettuce or other lettuce

Instructions

In a big skillet, heat the oil over medium-high heat.

Add the onions when the oil's surface begins to ripple. Sauté until transparent (3-4 minutes) (3-4 minutes).

When there is no longer any pink tint, add the ground turkey and simmer, stirring often. Break the turkey into little pieces while it cooks.

Stir in the salsa and taco seasoning after adding them. To enable the flavors to meld, cook for 1-2 minutes. Get rid of the heat.

Onto each big lettuce leaf, spoon 1/4 Cup of taco meat. Enjoy with chosen toppings!

Thai Chicken

Prep Time 20 Minutes

Cook Time 20 Minutes

Servings 4

Ingredients

- 4-5 boneless skinless thin, sliced chicken breasts
- Salt and black Pepper, to taste
- ½ Cup of Thai chili sauce
- 2 fresh limes juiced
- ¼ Cup of soy sauce
- 3 tbsp peanut butter
- 1 tbsp grated ginger
- 1 tbsp garlic

- Two bell peppers, red and orange, stemmed and chopped
- 1 Cup of broccoli, separated into florets
- 2 Cup of snow peas
- 1 Cup of carrots, sliced round
- ½ onion, diced
- 2 tbsp olive oil.
- Lime wheels, to top
- 1/4 Cup of peanuts, chopped.
- Fresh cilantro

Instructions

400 degrees Fahrenheit should be set for the oven.

In a large plastic bag that can be sealed, put the chicken.

Combine the peanut butter, lime juice, soy sauce, ginger, and garlic in a bowl, along with the sweet Thai chili sauce.

Blend by stirring.

Fill the bag with the chicken and sealable closure with 3/4 of the sauce.

Shake the bag before covering the chicken and letting it marinate for two hours.

Take the chicken out of the bag and set it on a baking sheet lined with parchment paper.

Add the peppers, broccoli, snow peas, carrots, and onion to a big bowl.

Add the remaining Thai peanut sauce and the olive oil.

Be sure to salt and pepper everything.

Place the lime wheels on top of the chicken and the veggies.

Bake the chicken for 20 minutes or until done.

Ensure that the veggies are soft.

The peanuts should be smashed and added to the dish.

Adding cilantro last.

Pineapple Chicken Stir-Fry

Prep Time 7 Minutes

Cook Time 15 Minutes

Total Time 22 Minutes

Ingredients

- ¼ Cup of soy sauce
- 2 tbsp sugar
- 1 tbsp cider vinegar
- 1 tbsp ketchup
- ½ tsp ginger
- 1 tbsp garlic –1 tsp
- 8 oz pineapple chunks drained; reserve 1/4 Cup of juice
- 1 lb boneless skinless chicken breast in 2 inch strips
- 2 tbsp vegetable oil
- 16 oz frozen stir fry vegetables
- hot cooked rice as needed

Instructions

Combine 1/4 cup of the saved pineapple juice with the soy sauce, sugar, vinegar, ketchup, ginger, chopped garlic, and cornstarch in a small bowl.

oil to the skillet Heat

Chicken is stir-fried in heated oil for approximately 5 minutes in a big pan. Add the frozen veggies and stir-fry for another 4 minutes.

The sauce and pineapple. Add stirring, then fully warm.

Over rice, please.

Easy Chicken Corn Chowder

Prep Time 25 Minutes

Cook Time 15 Minutes

Total Time 40 Minutes

Ingredients

- 1 Tsp butter
- ½ Cup of finely chopped onion
- ½ Cup of finely chopped celery
- 1 medium jalapeno pepper, seeded
- 2 Tsp all-purpose flour
- 3 Cup of 2% milk
- 2 Cup of chopped roasted skinless, boneless chicken breasts
- One 14.75-ounce can cream style corn
- 1½ Cup of frozen corn kernels (or 3 ears of fresh Corn)
- 1½ tsp chopped fresh thyme
- ½ tsp salt
- ⅛ tsp ground red pepper

Instructions

In a large saucepan set over medium heat, melt the butter. Add the onion, celery, and jalapeno; stir for 3 minutes or until cooked.

Add the flour and whisk continuously for 1 minutes. Add the milk and the other ingredients and stir.

To boil, then simmer until thickened (about 5 minutes.)

Chickpea & Feta Salad Recipe

Prep Time 20 Minutes

Cook Time 0 Minutes

Total Time 20 Minutes

Ingredients

- 2 Cup of canned chickpeas, rinsed and drained
- 1-2 garlic cloves, or to taste, finely
- 3 Tsp, thinly sliced scallions
- ½ large sweet red bell pepper, diced
- ½ Cup of diced English cucumber
- 2 Tsp fresh, finely parsley
- 9 large black or green olives, pitted and roughly chopped
- ½ Cup of crumbled feta cheese
- 3 Tsp fresh lemon juice
- 1 Tsp olive oil
- Salt and freshly ground black Pepper to taste
- 1 tsp lemon zest, for garnish (optional)

Instructions

The chickpeas, garlic, onions, red bell pepper, cucumber, parsley, olives, and feta cheese should all be combined in a medium bowl. Stir gently to mix.

After combining them in a small bowl, Over the chickpea mixture, drizzle some lemon juice and olive oil.

Use salt and Pepper to taste to season.

Cover and set in the refrigerator for at least 30 minutes to allow the flavors time to.

Serve with lemon zest as a garnish.

Egg roll in a bowl

Prep Time 20 Minutes

Cook Time 0 Minutes

Total Time 20 Minutes

Ingredients

- 1 tsp minced ginger
- 4 1/2 Cup of(s) packaged coleslaw mix (shredded cabbage and carrots)
- 1/2 Cup of(s) shredded carrots
- 3 medium scallions
- 3 Tbsp low sodium soy sauce
- 1 1/2 tsp sesame oil
- 1 pound(s) ground chicken breast (98% FF)

Instructions

Add the ginger after browning your preferred meat in a medium nonstick skillet until thoroughly done.

Add sesame oil and soy sauce.

Add the entire bag of slaw and mix to coat with the sauce.

Add a half Cup of shredded carrots, then toss them in the sauce.

Stir well, then add the chopped scallions. Cook over medium-high heat until the col slaw has reduced by half.

Serving Size: around 1 12 Cups of

Apples & Cranberries

Prep Time 10 Minutes

Cook Time 0 Minutes

Total Time 10 Minutes

Ingredients
- 2 ½ Cup of chopped cooked chicken
- 3 stalks of celery, chopped
- 1 Cup of chopped apple, about 1 large; I used a Pink Lady and kept the peel because it was organic
- ¼ Cup of dried cranberries
- ½ Cup of nonfat plain Greek yogurt
- 2 Tsp Hellman's light mayonnaise
- 2 tsp lemon juice
- 2 Tsp chopped parsley (optional)
- Salt and Pepper to taste

Instructions
Stir the chicken, celery, apple, and cranberries together in a bowl before setting it aside.

Combine the yogurt, mayonnaise, and lemon juice in a small bowl.

Stir thoroughly before adding it to the chicken mixture.

If preferred, stir in the parsley. Use salt and Pepper to taste to season.

SHEET PAN CHICKEN FAJITAS

Prep Time 10 Minutes

Cook Time 15 Minutes

Total Time 25 Minutes

Ingredients

- 1lb chicken, cut into thin strips
- ½ each- green, red, orange, and yellow bell pepper- thin sliced
- ½ red onion- thin sliced
- 1 Tsp olive oil
- 2 jalapeno- deseeded and diced
- 1 lime
- 8-10 6" Flour Tortillas
- Seasoning
- 1 tsp chili powder
- ¼ tsp cayenne
- 1 tsp paprika
- 1 tsp onion powder
- 1 tsp garlic powder
- 1 ½ tsp minced
- ½ tsp coriander
- 1 tsp sea salt & Pepper

Instructions

The oven to 425 degrees.

Add all of the fajita ingredients and 1 Tsp of olive oil to a bowl. Mix thoroughly.

Chicken and veggies are stirred in. Mix well to coat equally.

Avoid crowding the pan with too many pieces of chicken, or they won't get crispy.

Vegetables should be arranged around the pan's edges.

For 15 minutes, bake. For the final five minutes of the chicken's cooking, wrap the tortillas in foil and reheat them in the oven.

Cajun Chicken And Rice

Total Time 40 Minutes

Servings 4

Ingredients

- 1 tsp olive oil
- 1 clove garlic minced
- ½ green bell pepper chopped
- 1 onion chopped
- ½ tsp ground
- 1 tsp chili powder
- 2 tsp ca seasoning
- ⅓ Cup of long-grain brown rice
- ½ Cup of water
- 14½ oz canned stewed tomatoes
- 4 pimento-stuffed olives halved
- 1 Cup of cooked chicken cubed

Instructions

Oil should be heated at medium-high heat in a medium nonstick skillet.

Cook garlic, onion, and green Pepper over medium heat for about 8 minutes, turning often or until the veggies are soft.

Add Cajun spice, chili powder, and to the skillet. About 1 of stirring and cooking.

Place the rice in the skillet and constantly stir for about a or until the grains are coated.

Bring to a boil the tomatoes and water in the skillet.

For 15 minutes, simmer with the lid on.

Cook covered for approximately 5 minutes, or until chicken is hot and rice is done, in a pan with the olives.

Twice-Baked Potatoes

Prep Time 15 Minutes

Cook Time 10 Minutes

Total Time 25 Minutes

Ingredients
- 3 large baking potatoes
- ½ Cup of fat-free reduced-sodium chicken broth
- 1 Cup of 2% Milk Shredded Sharp Cheddar Cheese, divided
- 1/3 Cup of thin green onion slices
- ¼ Cup of Light Sour Cream
- 1 tsp Dijon Mustard
- ¼ tsp paprika

Instructions
The oven should be heated to 400°F.

Use the tip of a sharp knife to pierce potatoes numerous times. Until soft, bake for 1 to 1-1/2 hours. Potatoes should be immediately sliced in half lengthwise; scoop out the cores, leaving 1/4-inch-thick shells.

Thoroughly combine the potato pulp, broth, 1/2 Cup of cheese, onions, sour cream, and mustard with a mixer. Top with remaining cheese and paprika after spooning into the shells.

Bake for 20 minutes or until well heated.

Barbecue Chicken Tostada

Prep Time 10 Minutes

Cook Time 8 Minutes

Total Time 18 Minutes

Ingredients
- 8 tostada shells or 8 corn tortillas, brushed lightly with olive oil and baked for 3-5 minutes per side until crispy
- 3 a cup of sliced, cooked chicken
- 2/3 of a cup of your preferred barbecue sauce
- 2 Cup of shredded cheese (Mary uses mozzarella in the cookbook, but I have also used cheddar, Monterey Jack, or a blend)
- 3 green onions, very thinly sliced (optional)

Instructions
Set the oven to 350 °F. The tostada shells (baked tortillas) should be spread out on two rimmed baking pans.

In a small dish, mix the chicken with 1 Cup of barbecue sauce. Stir to coat.

After dividing the chicken between them, place a quarter cup of cheese on each tostada shell.

Just long enough for the cheese to melt in the oven, 6 to 8 minutes.

Take out of the oven and top with the final 1/2 cup of barbecue sauce. If desired, garnish with green onions.

Slow cooker taco soup

Cook Time 6 hr

Total Time 6 hr 10 Minutes

Ingredients
- 1b lean ground beef 96/4 or lean ground turkey
- 1 medium Onion, diced
- 1 1oz packet Low Sodium Ranch Dressing Mix such as Mrs. Dash *see notes
- 1 1oz packet Low Sodium Taco Seasoning such as Mrs. Dash *see notes
- 1 32 oz. box (low sodium) Swanson Chicken Broth
- 14.5 oz. can Tomato Sauce (low sodium)
- 2 - 14.5 oz cans Diced Tomatoes with Chiles
- 14.5 oz can Black Beans, drained (low sodium)
- 1 can Corn, drained (low sodium)
- Tortilla chips and added cheese for toppings - extra points

Instructions
Cook the onions and ground beef in a medium pan over medium heat. Remove any extra fat.

Combine the ground beef with the remaining ingredients and add to the slow cooker.

Cook for 4 hours on high or 6 hours on low.

Add some cheddar cheese and sour cream as a garnish.

Use the Sau setting on your Instant Pot to cook the onions and ground meat. Remove any fat. The remaining ingredients should be added to the Instant Pot.

Change to Pressure Cook mode and set the time to 20 minutes once that has finished cooking. Once the food is cooked, allow the pressure to relax gradually.

Size of serving: 1 Cup of.

Easy Chicken Pot Pie

Prep Time 5 Minutes

Cook Time 5 Minutes

Total Time 10 Minutes

Ingredients

- 1 2/3 Cup of Green Giant™ Steamers™ frozen mixed vegetables
- 1 Cup of cut-up cooked chicken
- 1 can (10 3/4 ounces) condensed cream of chicken soup
- 1 Cup of Original mix
- ½ Cup of milk
- 1 egg

Instructions

1 400F is the recommended temperature for the oven. Combine the veggies, chicken, and soup in a glass pie dish measuring 9 by 1 1/4 inches.

2 Utilizing a fork, mix the remaining ingredients. Into a pie dish, pour.

3 Until golden brown, bake for 30 minutes.

Baked Chicken with Lemon & Fresh Herbs

Total Time 45 Minutes

Prep Time 10 Minutes

Cook Time 35 Minutes

Serves 4

Ingredients

- 4 spray(s)
- 1 pound(s), four 4 oz halves
- ½ tsp
- ¼ tsp, freshly ground
- 1 tsp
- 2 tsp, fresh, chopped
- 2 tsp, chopped
- ¼ Cup of(s)
- ½ medium, quartered (for garnish)

Instructions

Set the oven to 400F. Spray cooking spray in a small, shallow roasting pan.

Chicken should be seasoned on all sides. Place chicken in the preheated pan; add oil, lemon juice, rosemary, and parsley on top. Pour broth over the chicken and down the sides of the pan.

Cook chicken in the oven for 30 to 35 minutes or until well done. Serve the food with a fresh lemon garnish.

One chicken breast half per serving.

GRILLED CILANTRO LIME SHRIMP KEBABS

Total Time 30 Minutes

Prep Time 25 Minutes

Cook Time 5 Minutes

- ## Ingredients
- 32 jumbo raw shrimp, peeled and deveined (17.5 oz after peeled)
- 3 cloves garlic, crushed
- 24 slices about 3 large limes, very thinly sliced into rounds (optional)
- olive oil cooking spray, I use my mister
- 1 tsp kosher salt
- 1 ½ tsp ground
- ¼ Cup of chopped fresh cilantro, divided
- 16 bamboo skewers soaked in water for 1 hour
- 1 lime cut into 8 wedges

Instructions

Spray oil on the grill's grates and heat it to medium heat.

Mix the shrimp with the garlic, salt, and half of the cilantro in a medium bowl.

Thread the shrimp and folded lime slices onto 8 pairs of parallel skewers, starting and finishing with the shrimp, to form 8 kebabs.

Grill the shrimp on each side for 1 to 2 minutes, turning them regularly until they are opaque.

Before serving, sprinkle the remaining cilantro and lime juice over the top.

crock pot salsa chicken

Total Time 44 Minutes

Cook Time 4 ½ Hrs

Ingredients

- 4 large boneless, skinless chicken breasts
- Salt and Pepper
- 2 Cup of favorite salsa

Instructions

After adding the chicken breasts to the slow cooker, season them with salt and Pepper, and then completely cover them with salsa. The crock pot has to be on low for 4 1/2 hours.

Place the chicken in a bowl and squeeze off the salsa but leave the liquid behind. Utilizing two forks, shred chicken; combine with strained salsa. Enjoy!

other ingredients are added. Enjoy.

One-Skillet Chicken and Broccoli Dinner

Prep Time 10 Minutes

Cook Time 30 Minutes

Total Time 40 Minutes

Ingredients

- 1 Tsp extra virgin olive oil
- 12 to 18 ounces of big, bite-sized chunks of boneless, skinless chicken breasts
- 2 Cup of broccoli florets
- 2 garlic cloves
- 1/2 Cup of yellow onion chopped
- 1/2 Cup of celery sliced
- 1/4 Cup of chicken broth or water
- 1/4 tsp kosher or sea salt
- 1/4 tsp black pepper
- Sauce
- 1/4 Cup of coconut optional tamari or lite soy sauce
- 2 Tsp vegetable

Instructions

Cook the chicken in a skillet with olive oil over medium heat for about 8 minutes. Remove and reserve the chicken. Broccoli florets should be added and lightly sautéed until just tender. Set aside broccoli after removing it.

Cook the onion and celery in the skillet for 5 to 8 minutes until the onion is transparent and softened. 30 seconds later, add the garlic and stir until fragrant. Add the salt and Pepper to the skillet and the chicken, broccoli, and broth (or water). Cook the mixture for a further five minutes, at most, until the chicken is well heated.

Mix the ingredients for the sauce in a bowl, then add it to the pan for the final of cooking. Dispense and savor!

Chili Cornbread Bake

Prep Time 15 Minutes

Cook Time 10 Minutes

Total Time 25 Minutes

Ingredients

- 1 (14.5 ounces) can of cream-style Corn
- 1/8 tsp + ¼ tsp ground cayenne pepper, divided
- 1 large egg, lightly beaten
- ¾ pounds 95% lean ground beef
- 1/3 Cup of skim milk
- 2 tsp ground, divided
- 1 (4 ounces) can dice green chiles, drained
- 1 garlic clove,
- 1 (8.5 ounces) box Jiffy corn muffin mix
- 1 small onion, diced
- ¾ Cup of canned kidney beans drained and rinsed
- 1 (14.5 ounces) can of diced tomatoes
- 2 tbsp chili powder
- ½ tsp salt
- 3 ounce 50% reduced fat Sharp Cheddar cheese, shredded

Instructions

Set the oven to 400 degrees. Spray a 9x13 baking dish with nonstick cooking spray to prepare it, then set it aside.

Mix the egg, milk, 1/8 tsp cayenne, 1 tsp, creamed Corn, chopped chilies, and corn muffin mix in a large mixing basin.

The mixture should be poured into the baking dish and smoothed into a uniform layer. Bake for 18 to 20 minutes, or until the tester emerges clean.

In the meantime, preheat a big skillet to medium heat. Add the ground beef when heated, breaking it into little pieces, and sauté for a bit.

Bits until they are just browned. Sauté the onions and garlic for two minutes or until aromatic.

Add the remaining 1 tsp of, 1/4 tsp of cayenne, chili powder, kidney beans, diced tomatoes, salt, and chili powder to the meat mixture. Stir until well blended and just thickened.

Remove the lid, turn the heat low, and simmer for five minutes.

With a fork, pierce the layer of cornbread, and then scoop the chili mixture over the top. Add the cheddar cheese to the chili, put it back in the oven, then 15 minutes of baking, or until the cheese has melted.

Has eight servings.

Chicken with Cider and Bacon Sauce

Prep Time 20 Minutes

Cook Time 25 Minutes

Total Time 45 Minutes

Ingredients

- Four 6-ounce skinless, boneless chicken breast halves
- ¼ tsp salt
- ¼ tsp freshly ground black Pepper
- 2 slices bacon, finely chopped
- ¼ Cup of finely chopped sweet onion
- ¾ Cup of unsweetened apple cider
- ½ Cup of fat-free, lower-sodium chicken broth

Instructions

Each chicken breast half should be placed between two sheets of heavy-duty plastic wrap (or wax paper), then pounded with a rolling pin or meat mallet to a thickness of 12 inches. Salt and Pepper should be uniformly distributed on the chicken.

In a large nonstick pan set over medium heat, cook the bacon until crisp. From the pan, remove the bacon. When the chicken is ready, add it to the pan drippings and cook for 6 minutes on each side. To keep warm, take the chicken out of the pan and wrap it in foil.

Add the onion to the pan and stir continuously for 2 minutes or until the onion is soft. Add the cider and broth, then boil while scraping any browned pieces from the bottom of the pan. Cook the broth combination until it is left with 1/2 cup (about 5 minutes). Add the cooked bacon and stir. Reheat the chicken by placing it back in the pan with the sauce spooned over it. Over the chicken, serve the sauce.

Thai Curry Chicken

Ingredients

- 1¼ pounds boneless skinless chicken breast, sliced into ½ -inch thick strips
- ¼ tsp salt
- 2 Tsp canola or vegetable oil, divided
- 1/2 Cup of thinly sliced shallots
- 8 ounces thin green beans or haricot verts, trimmed
- One medium red bell pepper, seeded and cut into thin strips
- 1 Cup of low-sodium chicken broth
- 1 Cup of canned light coconut milk
- 1 Tsp Thai red curry paste
- 1 Tsp Thai fish sauce
- 3 Cup of cooked brown rice (see Recipe Notes below)
- 2 Cup of baby spinach leaves, coarsely chopped
- 2 Tsp freshly squeezed lime juice
- ¼ Cup of fresh cilantro leaves

Instructions

Add salt to the chicken's seasoning. Over medium-high heat, warm 1 Tsp of the oil in a big skillet. Cook the chicken for approximately 5 minutes, tossing it periodically until it is barely cooked. Place the chicken in a large bowl.

The remaining Tsp of oil should be added to the pan. Add the shallots, green beans, and bell pepper and cook, occasionally turning, for about 3 minutes or until the veggies are crisp-tender. While boiling the veggies, add a splash of the chicken stock if the pan looks to dry. Add the veg to the bowl containing the chicken.

Stirring constantly, bringing the mixture to a mild boil while adding the fish sauce, coconut milk, chicken broth, and curry paste. For approximately 6 minutes, simmer the sauce over medium heat until it is reduced to about 114 Cup.

When heating packaged pre-cooked rice, go by the instructions on the package.

Return the chicken and veggies to the skillet once the sauce has been reduced, and simmer for 2 minutes more to reheat. After adding the spinach and lime juice, simmer for 30 seconds or until the spinach has just wilted. Serve in dishes with rice and cilantro on top.

Doritos Taco Salad

Prep Time 10 Minutes

Cook Time 8 Minutes

Total Time 18 Minutes

Ingredients

- 1 lb 95% lean ground beef
- 1 (1.25 oz) packet of reduced sodium taco seasoning
- 1 medium-large head of iceberg lettuce, chopped into bite-sized pieces (if you've never chopped up a head of an iceberg before, you can follow these directions)
- 1 medium-large tomato, diced
- 4 oz 50% less fat or 2% sharp cheddar cheese, shredded (such as Cabot)
- 4 oz nacho cheese Doritos, broken up a bit into bite-sized pieces
- 1 Cup of light Catalina or French dressing (I used Kraft Lite Catalina)

Instructions

Using a wooden spoon to split the ground beef into smaller pieces, brown it in a pan over medium heat. Stir in the taco spice packet until thoroughly combined. Place aside.

In a large dish, combine the lettuce, tomatoes, cheese, and ground beef. Add the Doritos and dressing when ready to serve, then toss to combine.

4 people that use Weight Watchers Per serving of a side dish (one Cup of), SmartPoints.

Per serving of a side dish (1 Cup of), there are 150 calories, 14 grams of carbohydrates, 6 grams of fat, 10 grams of protein, and 1 gram of fiber.

Skinny Meatloaf

Prep Time 15 Minutes

Bake Time 50 Minutes

Total Time 1 hour 15 Minutes

Ingredients

- 1 pound 96% extra lean ground beef. See shopping tips
- 1½ slices whole wheat bread remove crusts (I used Milton's Multigrain bread)
- 1 Cup of chopped onions
- 2 egg whites or 1 large egg
- 3 Tsp ketchup
- 1 Tsp spicy brown or yellow mustard
- 1 Tsp Worcestershire sauce
- ¼ tsp salt
- Fresh ground pepper to taste

Instructions

Turn the oven on to 350 degrees. Foil a baking sheet and set it aside.

Include the ground beef in a sizable bowl.

Remove the crust from the bread, mash it up, and put it in a food processor or blender to produce bread crumbs. Process the bread until it resembles crumbs.

To taste, bread crumbs, onions, egg whites, ketchup, mustard, Worcestershire sauce, salt, and Pepper should all be combined with the meat. Combine all the ingredients using your hands.

By hand, shape a loaf out of the meat mixture and place it on the baking pan. It needs to measure around 12" x 4."

The ingredients for the topping should be combined in a small dish. Cover the top of the meatloaf completely.

For 55 minutes, bake. Before slicing, remove from the oven and cool for at least 10 minutes. Slice into ten pieces.

It yields 5 servings. 2 slices per serving.

Burrito Bowl

Prep Time 10 Minutes

Cook Time 35 Minutes

Total Time 45 Minutes

Ingredients

- 1 medium onion finely chopped
- 1 medium bell pepper finely chopped
- 1 tsp onion powder/granules
- 1 tsp garlic powder/granules
- 1 tsp dried oregano
- 2 tsp ground
- 1.5 tsp paprika
- 0.5 tsp cayenne pepper
- 0.5 tsp salt
- 0.25 tsp ground black pepper
- 1 tbsp vegetable oil
- 16 oz ground beef - 5% fat (450g)
- 1 can black beans 1 x 15oz / 425g can (drained)
- 1 can sweetcorn 1 x 8.5oz / 248g can (drained)
- 1 can diced tomatoes 1 x 15oz / 425g can
- 1 Cup of rice (*brown if following Purple plan) (200g)
- 1 stock cube/bouillon cube, either beef or vegetable
- 2 Cup of water (240ml)

Instructions

Cut the Pepper and onion into tiny pieces and set them aside.

In a small bowl, combine the salt, Pepper, Cayenne Pepper, oregano, paprika, and onion powder. Set this mixture aside.

In a large skillet set over medium heat, warm the oil.

When the onions and peppers are tender, add them and cook, often stirring, for 6 to 8 minutes.

Add the ground beef and smash it with a wooden spoon or fork.

Cook the steak for 6 to 8 minutes, until it is well cooked and no longer pink.

Before adding the beans, Corn, and canned tomatoes, add the spice mixture, stir, and heat for one.

Stir well to mix everything thoroughly.

Add the stock cube or bouillon after dissolving it in two cups of boiling water.

Rice is lastly stirred in.

Stir well before bringing the mixture to a boil.

Reduce the heat, then let the rice simmer slowly for 15 to 20 minutes, frequently stirring to keep it from sticking to the pan or until the rice has absorbed most of the liquid.

Serve hot after being taken off the heat.

Enjoy!

Scrumptious Chicken Fried Rice

Prep Time 5 Minutes

Cook Time 5 Minutes

Total Time 10 Minutes

Ingredients

- 1½ Cup of cooked chicken breast, skinless and diced
- 3½ Cup of cooked brown rice. You can use about 1 Cup of raw Basmati brown rice
- 1½ tbsp canola oil
- 1 Cup of frozen peas, unthawed
- ½ Cup of sliced scallions
- 2 tsp toasted sesame oil or canola oil
- 1 Cup of chopped celery
- 3 tbsp low-sodium soy sauce
- 4 egg whites
- 2 scallions for garnish (optional)
- Black Pepper, to taste

Instructions

A big nonstick pan or wok should be filled with canola oil and heated over medium-high heat. Add the scallions and cooked chicken, and stir-fry for approximately.

Soy sauce, cooked rice, celery, and broken frozen peas should all be added. Stir gently to coat all ingredients and heat through after about 3 minutes of cooking. Place the rice mixture on the pan or wok's sides. Place egg whites in the wok's middle. Cook while circling the pan

1 or until the egg whites are thoroughly cooked. Rice mixture and eggs should be combined. Add a little black pepper and sesame oil before stirring everything together.

You are ready to serve now. For the following two days, leftovers can be kept in the refrigerator.

Scrumptious Chicken Fried Rice

Prep Time 5 Minutes

Cook Time 5 Minutes

Total Time 10 Minutes

Ingredients

- 1½ Cup of cooked chicken breast, skinless and diced
- 3½ Cup of cooked brown rice. You can use about 1 Cup of raw Basmati brown rice
- 1½ tbsp canola oil
- 1 Cup of frozen peas, unthawed
- ½ Cup of sliced scallions
- 2 tsp toasted sesame oil or canola oil
- 1 Cup of chopped celery
- 3 tbsp low-sodium soy sauce
- 4 egg whites
- 2 scallions for garnish (optional)
- Black Pepper, to taste

Instructions

A big nonstick pan or wok should be filled with canola oil and heated over medium-high heat. Add the scallions and cooked chicken, and stir-fry for approximately a.

Soy sauce, cooked rice, celery, and broken frozen peas should all be added. Stir gently to coat all ingredients and heat through after about 3 minutes of cooking. Place the rice mixture on the pan or wok's sides. Place egg whites in the wok's middle. The egg whites should be thoroughly cooked after about a of stirring. Rice mixture and eggs should be combined. Add a little black pepper and sesame oil before stirring everything together.

You are ready to serve now. For the following two days, leftovers can be kept in the refrigerator.

SKINNY GENERAL TSO'S CHICKEN

Prep Time 5 Minutes

Cook Time 5 Minutes

Total Time 10 Minutes

Ingredients

- 3/4 Cup of reduced-sodium chicken broth
- 2 tbsp cornstarch
- 2 tbsp sweetener (sugar substitute)
- 2 tbsp soy sauce
- 1 tbsp white wine vinegar
- 1/2 tsp ground ginger
- 2 tsp olive oil
- 2 scallion medium, chopped
- 2 tsp garlic
- 1/2 tsp red pepper flakes
- 1 lb boneless, skinless chicken breast
- 2 Cup of brown rice cooked

Instructions

Give the chicken 2 inch chunks.

In a small bowl, combine the chicken broth, cornstarch, Splenda, soy sauce, vinegar, and ginger. Place aside.

In a skillet or wok, heat the oil over medium-high heat. Add Pepper, garlic, and scallions. Simmer for two minutes, add the chicken and cook for five minutes, or until browned.

The chicken should be well cooked, about 3 minutes after adding the sauce. Over rice, serve the chicken and sauce.

Slow Cooker Shredded Korean Pork

Prep Time 10 Minutes

Cook Time 8 Hours

Total Time 8 Hours, 10 Minutes

Ingredients

- 3 lb lean pork tenderloin
- 1/3 Cup of brown sugar (or Stevia)
- 1/3 Cup of low-sodium soy sauce
- 10 cloves garlic, whole
- 1/2 Cup of red onion, diced
- 2 jalapenos, diced (or substitute 2-4 tbsp. Sriracha)
- 2 tbsp. fresh ginger root, peeled and grated
- 1 tbsp rice wine vinegar
- 2 tbsp sesame seeds

Instructions

Mix the sugar, soy sauce, red onion, jalapenos, ginger, rice vinegar, and sesame seeds in a separate bowl.

Pour the sauce over the meat and garlic in the slow cooker.

Cook on low for eight hours. Break the pork into more significant pieces when it has 30 minutes left to cook, and it is simple to shred with a fork. The sauce will thicken as it cooks without a cover. Completely shred the meat.

Oreo fluff

Prep Time 5 Minutes

Cook Time 5 Minutes

Total Time 10 Minutes

Ingredients

- 1 1oz box
- instant vanilla pudding mix (Sugar-Free)
- 2 Cup of skim milk
- 1 (8 oz) container of Fat-Free Cool Whip
- 6 reduced-fat Oreos, crushed

Instructions

Milk and pudding mix are whisked for 2 minutes in a big bowl. Combine the Oreos and cool whip.

The bowl should be covered with plastic wrap and chill overnight or for 1 hour until the fluff has set.

10 servings; each one is a heaping ½ Cup of.

Spice Cake Mix Minutesi Muffins

Prep Time 10 Minutes

Cook Time 12 Minutes

Total Time 22 Minutes

Ingredients

- 1 box (15 - 18 ounces) spice cake mix (I substituted a yellow cake mix with
- 1 Tsp pumpkin pie spice whisked in)
- 1 can (15 ounces) of canned pumpkin puree

Instructions

Place an oven rack in the oven's middle.

Mix muffins may be made by preheating the oven to 400F and lining 24 mix muffin tins with paper liners or nonstick spray. (You may also make more regular muffins in standard pans.)

Ignoring the directions on the cake mix, combine the two ingredients to make the batter in a big basin. The mixture will be pretty thick and will require some work.

Assemble the batter in the micro muffin Cup of pans, dividing it equally.

Bake the Mix-muffins for 10 to 12 minutes at 400 degrees Fahrenheit or until a toothpick inserted in the center comes clean.

Take out and cool on wire racks.

Skinny One Point Weight Watcher Pancakes

Prep Time 10 Minutes

Cook Time 10 Minutes

Total Time 4 Minutes

Ingredients
- 2 over-ripe bananas mashed
- 2 egg whites
- 1 Cup of fat-free plain greek yogurt
- 1/2 Cup of fat-free milk
- 1 tsp of pure vanilla extract
- 1 Cup of all-purpose flour
- 2 tsp of baking powder
- 1/2 tsp of cinnamon

Instructions
A nonstick electric skillet should be heated to 325 degrees.

Mash bananas, egg whites, Greek yogurt, milk, and vanilla essence should all be combined in a medium bowl. Stir everything together thoroughly.

Flour, baking powder, and cinnamon should be combined and whisked in an enormous basin.

Mix wet and dry components.

A heated skillet should have ¼ Cup of batter in it. Cook until golden brown.

Chicken Enchilada Bake

Prep Time 30 Minutes

Cook Time 30 Minutes

Total Time 1 hr

Ingredients
- 19-ounce enchilada sauce canned
- 9 extra thin yellow corn tortillas
- 16-ounce fat-free refried beans can
- 1 packet of taco seasoning or the equivalent of homemade taco seasoning
- 1.5 pounds boneless skinless chicken breasts COOKED and chopped into small pieces
- 1 Cup of black beans drained and rinsed
- 1 can diced tomatoes and green chilies drained
- 1 Cup of 2% shredded fiesta cheese

Instructions
Set oven to 350 degrees Fahrenheit.

Apply nonstick cooking spray to a 9 x 13 baking dish.

The bottom of the pan should be covered with 1/3 Cup of the enchilada sauce.

Spread 4.5 tortillas on the pan's bottom to cover it completely.

Refried beans and taco seasoning should be combined in a dish.

On top of the corn tortillas, evenly distribute this mixture.

Add the cooked chicken, black beans, tomatoes/chilies, and leftover enchilada sauce to the same bowl. Combine these components by stirring.

Place a layer of refried beans on top of half of this mixture.

On top of the layers, place the remaining 4.5 corn tortillas.

Spread the leftover chicken mixture equally over the corn tortillas.

Cheese should be added on top.

For around 30 minutes, bake.

Honey Garlic Pork Chops Recipe

Prep Time 10 Minutes

Cook Time 15 Minutes

Total Time 25 Minutes

Ingredients
- 2 tbsp low-sodium soy sauce
- ½ Cup of ketchup
- 2 cloves crushed garlic
- 2⅔ tbsp honey
- 6 (4oz each) 1-inch thick pork chops

Instructions
Turn the grill on either inside or outside to medium heat.

Lightly oil the grill grates to prepare them.

Add soy sauce, ketchup, garlic, and honey to a medium mixing bowl.

Mixing the materials.

Sear the pork chops on both sides on the preheated grill.

Lightly apply the prepared glaze to all surfaces using a basting brush.

The pork chops should be grilled for 8 minutes on each side until the insides are no longer pink and an instant-read thermometer reads 145° F when inserted into the chop.

Taco fiesta bubble-up casserole

Prep Time 20 Minutes

Cook Time 50 Minutes

Total Time 1 hr 10 Minutes

Ingredients

- 1 lb cooked extra lean ground beef
- 1 7.5 oz package of Pillsbury biscuits (10 biscuits to the pack, the ones In the 4 value pack, if you can't find that Size, you can buy the bigger Size and weigh it out)
- 1 package Taco seasoning, 30g
- 1 1/3 Cups of salsa
- 2 Cup of diced peppers I used red, orange and yellow
- 1 Cup of diced onion. I used red onion.
- 1 Cup of reduced-fat shredded cheese. I use a 3 cheese blend.
- Green onion
- Fat-free sour cream for topping optional

Instructions

Taco seasoning is added to the ground beef after cooking in a skillet on the stove.

Spray a 9x13 casserole dish with cooking spray, then preheat the oven to 350°F.

In a bowl, combine the salsa and the ground beef.

After chopping the peppers, onion, and biscuits into six pieces.

Layer half of the biscuit pieces in the bottom of the casserole dish. On top of those, layer half of the meat mixture, half of the peppers and onions, and half of the cheese. Continue layering and top with the finely chopped green onion.

Wrap loosely in foil and bake for 35 minutes, then take off the foil and bake for 15 minutes. After 5 minutes of cooling, slice into 6 halves. Eight personal points per serving, which is 7 standard or 6 extra. Add a spoonful of sour cream without fat on top (optional)

Printed in Great Britain
by Amazon

35743465R00077